THE DESTRUCTION OF ANCIENT ROME

THE DESTRUCTION OF

ANCIENT ROME

A Sketch of the History of the Monuments

RODOLFO LANCIANI

ARNO PRESS
A New York Times Company
New York • 1980

First published 1901
Reissued 1967 by Benjamin Blom, Inc.

Reprint Edition 1980
LC 80-933
ISBN 0-405-08726-8
Manufactured in the United States of America

PREFATORY NOTE

PROFESSOR RODOLFO LANCIANI needs no introduction to English readers.

This book sums up briefly the results of researches, extending over many years, in regard to the fate of the buildings and masterpieces of art in ancient Rome. In his work upon this subject and upon his large map Professor Lanciani has searched hundreds of volumes of municipal and ecclesiastical records, besides examining several thousand separate documents; and he has ransacked the principal libraries of Europe for prints and drawings showing the remains of ancient Rome at different periods. Much of the new material thus collected will appear in fuller form in an extensive work, comprising several volumes, which will be published in Italian under the title *Storia degli Scavi di Roma*. The present volume is a forerunner of the larger work.

Thanks are due to Professor Walter Dennison of Oberlin College, for kind assistance in reading the proofs, and for the compilation of the Indexes.

F. W. K.

NOVEMBER 1, 1899.

CONTENTS

CHAPTER		PAGE
I.	The Destroyers of Ancient Rome	3
II.	The Transformation of Republican Rome by the Emperors	10
III.	The Use of Earlier Materials, particularly Marbles, in the Building Operations of the Later Empire	28
IV.	The Aspect of the City at the Beginning of the Fifth Century	47
V.	The Sack of the Goths in 410, and its Consequences	56
VI.	The Sack of Rome by the Vandals in 455	74
VII.	The City in the Sixth Century	77
VIII.	Burial Places within and without the Walls	89
IX.	The Devastation and Desertion of the Campagna	101
X.	The Monuments in the Seventh Century	106
XI.	The Incursion of the Saracens in 846, and the Extension of the Fortifications of the City	126
XII.	The Flood of 856	139
XIII.	The Rome of the Einsiedlen Itinerary	142
XIV.	The Usurpers of the Holy See and the Sack of 1084	154
XV.	Rome at the End of the Twelfth Century — The Itinerary of Benedict	174

CONTENTS

CHAPTER		PAGE
XVI.	Marble-cutters and Lime-burners of Mediaeval and Renaissance Rome	180
XVII.	The Beginnings of the Modern City	198
XVIII.	The Sacking of Rome by the Army of Charles of Bourbon in 1527	214
XIX.	The Monuments in the Latter Part of the Sixteenth Century	227
XX.	The Modernisation of Mediaeval Buildings in the Seventeenth and Eighteenth Centuries	253
XXI.	Modern Use of Ancient Materials	258

INDEXES:

I.	Index of Subjects	267
II.	Index of Passages and Inscriptions	278

LIST OF ILLUSTRATIONS

Panoramic view of Rome by Balthasar Jenichen . . *Frontispiece*

FIGURE		PAGE
1.	Substructions of the palace of Septimius Severus. From a photograph	2
2.	Torre dei Schiavi. From a photograph	6
3.	Section of steps of the round temple of the Forum Boarium, showing earlier and later construction	11
4.	Fragment of painted terra cotta antefix from the temple of Jupiter Optimus Maximus. From Tav. xiii. of the *Bullettino Comunale*, 1896	12
5.	Fragment of painted tile from an early temple on the Esquiline. From Tav. xiii. of the *Bullettino Comunale*, 1896	13
6.	Section of excavations in the Via di S. Gregorio, showing changes of level	19
7.	Fragment of the tomb of Celer. From a photograph	21
8.	Excavation of the Via Nazionale on the Quirinal, showing remains of buildings of different periods. From a photograph	25
9.	Part of the upper story of the Coliseum, repaired with materials from earlier buildings. From a photograph	29
10.	Another view of the upper story of the Coliseum, showing repairs made with architectural fragments from various sources. From a photograph	30
11.	A statue, broken into fragments, in process of reconstruction. From a photograph	44
12.	The monument of Stilicho in the Forum. From a photograph	51
13.	The raising of level at the Porta Ostiensis, A.D. 402	54
14.	Bronze heads found in 1880 under the English Church, Via del Babuino. After Tav. i. of the *Bullettino Comunale*, 1881	67
15.	Section of the channel of the Aqua Marcia, at Monte Arcese, showing deposits on the bottom and sides	81
16.	The remains of the Claudian aqueduct at the Porta Furba. From a photograph	86

LIST OF ILLUSTRATIONS

FIGURE		PAGE
17.	Tomb of P. Vibius Marianus, so-called "Tomb of Nero," on the Via Clodia, 4½ miles north of Rome. From a print	93
18.	Columbarium on the Via Severiana, near Ostia, opened in 1868. From a print	94
19.	The Sepolcro degli Stucchi, showing the hole made by plunderers in the vaulted ceiling. From a print	97
20.	View of the Campagna, remains of the Claudian aqueduct in the distance. From a photograph	100
21.	The column of Phocas in the Forum. From a photograph	107
22.	The Pronaos of the Pantheon. From a photograph	113
23.	The tomb of St. Paul and the canopy of Arnolfo di Lapo in S. Paolo fuori le Mura, after the fire of 1823. From a print	132
24.	Tower of the wall of Leo IV., now used as an observatory. From a photograph	134
25.	The Forum flooded by the Tiber, 1898. From a photograph	140
26.	The Ponte Salario, two miles north of Rome; blown up to prevent the advance of Garibaldi in 1867. From a photograph	149
27.	View of the Caelian hill, looking southeast. From a photograph	163
28.	View of the Forum in 1821, partly excavated, showing the difference between the ancient and the modern level. From an engraving	167
29.	The obelisk of the gardens of Sallust as it lay after it had fallen. From a sketch by Fontana	171
30.	The lower end of the obelisk of the Campus Martius. From a sketch by Bandini	172
31.	A typical Roman house of the twelfth century, built with odd fragments. From a photograph	179
32.	The pulpit in the cathedral of S. Mattéo at Salerno, built with marbles from Rome. From a photograph	185
33.	Fragments of cornice from the temple of Vulcan at Ostia. From a photograph	195
34.	House and tower of the Margani. From a photograph	200
35.	A lane of Mediaeval Rome — Via della Lungarina, demolished in 1877. From a photograph	202
36.	The Porta del Popolo of the time of Sixtus IV. From a sketch by M. Heemskerk (1536)	209
37.	Reliefs from the tomb of Calpurnianus, the charioteer. From a photograph	210

LIST OF ILLUSTRATIONS

FIGURE		PAGE
38.	The hill of S. Onofrio, where Charles of Bourbon established his headquarters. From a photograph	215
39.	One of the Sale Borgia — that of the "Vita della Madonna" — in the Vatican. From a photograph	223
40.	Bas-reliefs from the arch of Marcus Aurelius, now in the Conservatori Palace. From a photograph	229
41.	The statues of Castor and Pollux on the Capitoline hill, restored in 1584. From a photograph	233
42.	View of the Lateran buildings before their destruction by Sixtus V. From a sketch by Ciampini	243
43.	The Loggia of Pietro Squarcialupi, Palazzo del Senatore. From an old print	248
44.	The Ponte Rotto, half carried away by the inundation of 1557. From a photograph	249
45.	The Cesi chapel in the church of S. Maria della Pace, built with Pentelic marble from the temple of Jupiter Optimus Maximus. From a photograph	260

SELECT BIBLIOGRAPHY

HISTORICAL AND TOPOGRAPHICAL WORKS

Adinolfi, Pasquale: Roma nell' età di mezzo. 2 vols. Rome, 1881.

Armellini, Mariano: Le chiese di Roma dal Secolo IV. al XIX. 2d edit., Rome, 1891.

Corpus Inscriptionum Latinarum: Vols. VI., 1876 sq., and XIV., 1887.

De Rossi, Giovanni Battista: Inscriptiones Christianae Urbis Romae saeculo septimo antiquiores. Rome, Vol. I., 1861; Vol. II., pars 1, 1888.

―― Roma Sotterranea Cristiana. Vol. I., 1864.

―― Roma Sotterranea; or, Some Account of the Roman Catacombs. Translated by J. S. Northcote and W. R. Brownlow. London, 1869. New ed., 1879.

Duchesne, Louis: Le Liber Pontificalis — Texte, introduction et commentaire par l'abbé L. Duchesne. 2 vols. Paris, 1886–1892.

Dyer, Thomas H.: A History of the City of Rome, its Structures and Monuments. London, 1865.

Gibbon, Edward: History of the Decline and Fall of the Roman Empire.

Gilbert, O.: Geschichte und Topographie der Stadt Rom im Alterthum. Leipzig, 3 parts, 1883, 1885, 1890.

Gregorovius, Ferdinand: Geschichte der Stadt Rom im Mittelalter. 8 vols., 4th ed. Stuttgart, 1886–1896.

―― History of the City of Rome in the Middle Ages. Translated from the Fourth German edition by Annie Hamilton. Vols I.–VI. London, 1894–1899.

Grisar, Hartman, S. L.: Geschichte Roms und der Päpste im Mittelalter. Freiburg, Vol. I., 1898.

Helbig, Wolfgang: Guide to the Public Collections of Classical Antiquities in Rome. Translation by J. F. and F. Muirhead. 2 vols. Leipzig, 1895–1896.

Jaffè, Phil.: Regesta Pontificum romanorum ab condita ecclesia ad ann. 1198. 2d ed., revised by Kaltenbrunner, etc. 2 vols. Leipzig, 1885–1888.

Jordan, H.: Topographie der Stadt Rom im Alterthum. Berlin, Vol. I., part i., 1878, part ii., 1885; Vol. II., 1871.

Kraus, Franz Xavier: Geschichte der christlichen Kunst. Vol. I. Freiburg, 1896.

Lanciani, Rodolfo: Pagan and Christian Rome. Boston, 1893.

—— Ancient Rome in the Light of Recent Discoveries. Boston, 1888.

—— The Ruins and Excavations of Ancient Rome. Boston, 1897.

—— L' Itinerario di Einsiedlen e l' ordine di Benedetto Canonico. Rome, 1891.

—— I Commentarii di Frontino intorno le acque e gli acquedotti. Rome, 1880.

—— Forma Urbis Romae. Milan, 1893 sq. (XLVI sheets.)

Marangoni, Giovanni: Delle cose gentilesche e profane, trasportate ad uso ed ornamento delle chiese. Rome, 1744.

Mommsen, Theodore: Monumenta Germaniae historica: Gesta pontificum Romanorum. Vol. I. Berlin, 1898.

Müntz, Eugène: Les Arts à la cour des Papes. 3 vols. (To Sixtus IV.) Paris, 1878–1882.

—— Les Arts à la cour des Papes. (Innocent VIII.–Pius III.) Paris, 1898.

Muratori, Ludovico: Rerum Italicarum Scriptores.

Nichols, F. M.: The Marvels of Rome; or, A Picture of the Golden City. An English version of the Mediaeval Guidebook. London, 1889.

Richter, Otto: Topographie der Stadt Rom. Noerdlingen, 1889.

Tommasini, Oreste: Della storia medievale della Città di Roma e dei più recenti raccontatori di essa: in Archivio della Società Romana di Storia Patria, Vol. I., 1877.

Urlichs, C. L.: Codex urbis Romae topographicus. Würzburg, 1871.

PERIODICALS

Archivio della Società Romana di Storia Patria. Rome, from 1877.
Bullettino della Commissione archeologica comunale di Roma, from 1873.
Bullettino di Archeologia cristiana, edited by Giovanni Battista de Rossi, Vols. I.–XIII. Rome, 1863–1895.
Nuovo Bullettino di Archeologia cristiana, edited by G. B. de Rossi, E. Stevenson, O. Marucchi. Rome, from 1895.
Mittheilungen des Kaiserlich Deutschen Archaeologischen Instituts, Roemische Abtheilung; from 1886, following the *Annali* and *Bullettino*, 1829–1885.
La Civiltà Cattolica. Interesting contributions by H. Grisar. See also Grisar's Analecta Romana, Vol. I. Naples, 1899.
Mélanges de l'École française de Rome. Rome, from 1881. Interesting contributions by L. Duchesne.
Notizie degli Scavi di Antichità. Rome, from 1876.
Roemische Quartalschrift für Christliche Altertumskunde. Rome, from 1887.
Studii e Documenti di Storia e Diritto. Rome, from 1880.

FIG. 1. — Substructions of the palace of Septimius Severus.

DESTRUCTION OF ANCIENT ROME

CHAPTER I

THE DESTROYERS OF ANCIENT ROME

I WAS sitting not long ago at the southern extremity of the Palatine hill, where the remains of the palace of Septimius Severus tower a hundred and sixty feet above the level of the modern streets, and I was trying to fathom the abyss which lay open at my feet, and to reconstruct in imagination the former aspect of the place. By measurements on the spot, compared with descriptions and drawings left by those who saw the Palatine in a better state of preservation, I have been able to ascertain that a palace 490 feet long, 390 wide, and 160 high has so completely disappeared that only a few pieces of crumbling wall are left here and there against the cliff to tell the tale. Who broke up and removed, bit by bit, that mountain of masonry? Who overthrew the giant? Was it age, the elements, the hand of barbarians, or some other irresistible force the action of which has escaped observation?

To answer these questions we must first try to grasp the meaning of the words "destruction" and "disappearance" when applied to the monuments of ancient Rome. We are told, for instance, that 485,000 spectators could find room in the Circus Maximus, and that, when Trajan gave up to the people his own imperial balcony, the available space was increased by 5000 seats. Perhaps there is an exaggeration in these figures; in fact, the capacity of the Circus has been limited by Huelsen to 150,000 spectators.[1] But even with this reduction, we may suppose that here 150,000 persons sat on stone or marble benches which were made accessible by an elaborate system of stairways; if we allow to each spectator an average space of twenty inches, there must have been in the Circus Maximus more than 250,000 running feet of stone and marble benches. Not a fragment has come down to us, and we are left in complete ignorance as to the way in which so great a mass of solid material has disappeared.

Near the Pantheon of Agrippa, on the border of the pond or *stagnum* where Nero and Tigellinus used to feast in a floating hall, there was a colonnade known by the name of Eventus Bonus. Its site was unknown to topographers until May, 1891, when a capital of great size was discovered in the Vicolo del Melone, near the church of S. Andrea della Valle: so great, indeed, was that mass of marble that we were obliged to abandon it

[1] *Bullettino Comunale*, 1894, p. 322.

where it lay, on account of the danger of undermining the neighbouring houses if we should attempt to remove it. Whence came the great block? I found a clew to the answer in Flaminio Vacca's account of the excavations in the time of Pius IV. (1559-1566). "In laying the foundations of the Palazzo della Valle," says Vacca, "columns, fragments of entablatures, and other marbles were found, among them a capital of enormous size, out of which the coat of arms of the Pope on the Porta Pia was chiselled."[1] A second capital was discovered under the Ugolini house, in the Vicolo del Melone, in 1862; and a third, under the Palazzo Capranica della Valle in 1876. These three capitals and the one found in 1891 were lying on a line measuring 300 feet between the two outermost; they all belonged to a colonnade, the columns of which were 47 feet high, the capitals themselves being 6 feet high and 14 feet in circumference. The significance of these dimensions will best be appreciated by architects.

Ancient documents further mention a stadium (where now is the Piazza Navona) with seats for 30,088 spectators, an odeum (now the Monte Giordano) with 11,600 seats, the theatre of Balbus (now the Monte de' Cenci) with 11,510 seats, and the theatre of Pompey (near the

[1] *Memorie di varie antichità trovate in diversi luoghi . . . scritte da Flaminio Vacca nel 1594*, in Fea's *Miscellanea*, Vol. I. p. 25. Latest and best edition by Richter in *Berichte der Sächs. Gesellschaft der Wissenchaften*, 1881, p. 43.

Campo di Fiori) with 17,580 seats. Of all these marble and stone buildings, no traces are left above ground.

Examples of this kind are by no means confined to the area within the city walls. In the Life of the Emperor Gordianus the younger, chap. 32, a description

Fig. 2. — Torre dei Schiavi.

is given of his villa on the Via Praenestina, two and a half miles outside the gate of that name. It contained, among other buildings, a colonnade of two hundred columns, fifty of which were of cipollino or Carystian marble, fifty of portasanta, fifty of pavonazzetto or

Phrygian marble, and fifty of giallo antico or Numidian; there were also three basilicas, each a hundred feet long, an imperial palace, and baths which, in size and magnificence, rivalled the thermae of Rome itself. The present state of this Villa Gordianorum is shown in our illustration (Fig. 2). Colonnade, basilicas, palace, baths, — all have disappeared. One bit of ruin stands alone in the wilderness, a landmark for miles around, — the Torre dei Schiavi, a favourite meet of the foxhounds in the Campagna.

We may grant that natural agencies have contributed their share to the demolition of ancient buildings, — fires, floods, earthquakes, and the slow but resistless processes of disintegration due to rain, frost, and variations of temperature; but such prodigious changes, such wholesale destruction, could have been accomplished only by the hand of man.

Writers on the decline and fall of the Roman Empire have proposed several explanations, all of which are plausible; all contain elements of truth. But at the outset we may discard the current view that the disappearance of Roman monuments was due to the barbarians — as if these, in their meteoric inroads, could have amused themselves by pulverizing the 250,000 feet of stone and marble seats in the Circus, for example, or the massive structure of the villa of the Gordiani! The purpose of the barbarians was to carry off such articles of value as could easily be removed, and Rome long remained rich enough to satisfy their greed. Later, when this mine had become exhausted, and the houses of the living were stripped of all their valuables, they may have attacked the abodes of the dead, the humble catacombs of the faithful as well as the imperial mausoleums; but the stanch buildings of the Republic and of the Empire were not essentially damaged.

As we shall see in the course of our narrative, in June, 455 A.D., the temple of Jupiter Optimus Maximus on the Capitoline hill and the palace of the Caesars could still be successfully plundered of movable objects. In 536 the garrison of the mole of Hadrian, which had long ago been converted into a fortress (now the Castle of S. Angelo), was able to check an assault of the Goths by throwing down upon their heads the masterpieces of Greek art which still adorned the mausoleum. A quarter of a century later the historian Procopius states that many statues by Phidias and Lysippus could yet be seen in Rome.

In 630 Pope Honorius I., with the consent of the Emperor Heraclius, removed the gilt-bronze tiles from the roof of the temple of Venus and Rome, for the adornment of the roof of St. Peter's; the temple, therefore, was still intact. In 663, when Rome for the last time, and to her misfortune, was visited by an emperor, — a Christian emperor too, — a great deal was still left to plunder. In the brief period of twelve days which Constans spent in the city he removed many bronze statues, and laid his hands also upon the bronze tiles of the Pantheon, although this had long since been converted into a Christian church.

The barbarians, therefore, can be left in peace, their part in the destruction of Rome being hardly worth considering when compared with the guilt of others. By "others" I mean the Romans themselves, of the Imperial, Byzantine, Mediaeval, and Renaissance periods.

CHAPTER II

THE TRANSFORMATION OF REPUBLICAN ROME BY THE EMPERORS

THE growth of a city involves the readjustment of its edifices, public and private, to the needs of a population living under new conditions; and in a certain sense we may say that the history of the destruction of Rome begins with the reign of Augustus, who undertook to transform the capital of the Empire from a city of bricks into a city of marble. In widening and draining the old streets, in opening new thoroughfares, in building the new quarters, and in carrying out a general scheme for the sanitation and embellishment of the metropolis, many historical monuments were sacrificed. To clear the space for the erection of the theatre of Marcellus, for example, the shrine of Pietas was destroyed, so dear to the Romans on account of the legend of the faithful daughter who, with the milk of her breast, kept alive the father sentenced to death by starvation in the old Decemviral jail.[1] Dion Cassius adds that many houses and temples were demolished to make room for this structure; that many

---

[1] Pliny, *Hist. Nat.* VII. 36, 121.

statues of the gods, of ancient workmanship, carved in wood and stone, shared the fate of the temples; and that the builders of the theatre were suspected of having appropriated the gold and valuables stored away in the vaults (*favissae*) of the sacred edifices.[1]

The example set by Augustus was followed by his wealthy friends, Marcius Philippus, Lucius Cornificius, Cornelius Balbus, and Statilius Taurus; but Agrippa

FIG. 3. — Section of steps of the round temple of the Forum Boarium, showing earlier and later construction.

surpassed them all in the number and splendour of his buildings.[2] We may compare the work of these men with that of the popes and cardinals of the seventeenth century, who modernised our Constantinian and mediaeval churches; but there is this differ-

[1] Dion Cassius, XLIII. 49. [2] Suetonius, *Octav.* 29.

ence, that while the renovation of the seventeenth century was without excuse and had no redeeming feature, Augustus and his friends did, at least, substitute masterpieces of Greco-Roman construction, of the purest type, for the earlier structures of brick or rough stone.

This change may best be studied, perhaps, in the so-called temple of the Mater Matuta in the Forum Boarium, afterwards the church of S. Stefano delle Carozze, now S. Maria del Sole, in the Piazza Bocca della Verità. Here we see the stone steps leading to the stone cella of the time of Camillus, covered, but not entirely concealed, by the marble steps and the marble cella of the time of Augustus (Fig. 3). In excavating strata of rubbish of the time of Augustus, such as the platform of the Gardens of Maecenas, or that of the Capitolium, we have actually picked up fragments from temples of the time of the Kings, dumped there with

FIG. 4. — Fragment of painted terra cotta antefix from the temple of Jupiter Optimus Maximus.

other materials to raise the level of the ground. Such are the antefixes of painted terra cotta from the temple of Jupiter Optimus Maximus, now in the Palazzo de' Conservatori,[1] and the roof-tiles from another shrine on the Esquiline, in the Museo Municipale al Celio.[2] In the early centuries of Rome sacred edifices were built of wood, and ornamented with panels, cornices, and tiles of terra cotta with polychrome decoration. A structure of this kind was discovered on the site of Falerii, Città Castellana, in 1886; the remains of it are exhibited in one of the halls of the Villa di Giulio III., outside the Porta del Popolo.[3]

Fig. 5. — Fragment of painted tile from an early temple on the Esquiline.

In tracing the history of the destruction of the Rome of the Kings and of the Republic at the hands of the Emperors, three facts become prominent: (1) the complete covering over, for hygienic reasons, and conse-

---

[1] *Bull. Com.*, 1896, p. 187, Pl. xii.–xiii. (see Fig. 4).
[2] *Ibid.*, 1896, p. 28 (see Fig. 5).
[3] *Monumenti antichi publicati per cura della reale Accad. dei Lincei*, Vol. IV., 1895.

quent elevation, of large tracts of land; (2) the rebuilding, on a totally different plan, of one or more quarters of the City, after a destructive fire; and (3) the clearing of large areas to make room for the great thermae, — those of Nero, Titus, Trajan, Caracalla, the Decii, Diocletian, and Constantine.

The first record that we have of the covering over and elevation of a large area for hygienic reasons dates from the time of Augustus. A part of the Esquiline hill was occupied at that time by a "field of death," where the bodies of slaves and beggars and of criminals who had undergone capital punishment were thrown into common pits (*puticuli*), together with the carcasses of domestic animals and beasts of burden. In the excavations made in laying out the Via Napoleone III., in 1887, about seventy-five of these pits were discovered. In some of them the animal remains had been reduced to a uniform mass of black, unctuous matter; in others the bones so far retained their shape that they could be identified. The field of death served also as a dumping place for the daily refuse of the city.[1] This hotbed of infection was suppressed by Augustus at the suggestion of his prime minister Maecenas. The district was buried under fresh earth to the depth of 24 feet, and a public park, a fifth of a mile in extent, was laid out on the newly made ground. The results proved of so great benefit to the

[1] *Ancient Rome in the Light of Recent Discoveries*, p. 64.

health of the City that Horace thought the work worthy to be sung in verse. In the quaint, though by no means literal, translation of Francis (*Sat.* I. VIII. 8 *et seq.*) : —

>In coffins vile the herd of slaves
>Were hither brought to crowd their graves;
>And once in this detested ground
>A common tomb the vulgar found;
>Buffoons and spendthrifts, vile and base,
>Together rotted here in peace.
>A thousand feet the front extends,
>Three hundred deep in rear it bends,
>And yonder column plainly shows
>No more unto its heirs it goes.
>But now we breathe a purer air,
>And walk the sunny terrace fair,
>Where once the ground with bones was white, —
>With human bones, a ghastly sight!

In process of time recourse was had to the same expedient in the case of other cemeteries within or near the walls of Aurelian. The twenty-four million cubic feet of earth and rock, removed by Trajan from the west slope of the Quirinal to make room for his Forum, were spread over the cemetery between the Via Salaria Vetus (Pinciana) and the Via Salaria Nova.[1] The Licinian Gardens — a portion of the great imperial park on the Esquiline, formerly owned by the Licinian family — were laid out, likewise, on the site of the cemetery

[1] *Pagan and Christian Rome*, p. 284.

between the Via Collatina and Via Labicana. The same fate befell the beautiful burial-grounds of the Via Aurelia, now occupied by the Villa Corsini-Pamfili, near the Casino dei Quattro Venti.[1] No injury was done to the tombs when the earth was heaped upon them; their sacred character protected them from sacrilege, and the cinerary urns, the inscriptions, and the more or less valuable furniture of the sepulchres were left undisturbed. The excavation of these cemeteries in modern times has proved to be exceptionally rich in finds.

The vast conflagrations which from time to time swept over the city were in reality a means of improvement, both from the aesthetic and from the hygienic point of view. Such was the fire described by Livy in the twenty-seventh chapter of Book XXVI., by which all the shops and houses around the Forum, the residence of the high priest, the fish-market, and the buildings in the region of the Lautumiae were destroyed. The district was rebuilt on a better and more sanitary plan. This historian describes another fire (XXIV. 47), by which the region of the Forum Boarium, from the foot of the Aventine to the present Piazza Montanara, was devastated in 213 B.C.; and again in 192 B.C. the same quarter was burned over. I saw traces of the fires last mentioned in April, 1886, when the main

[1] *Pagan and Christian Rome*, p. 269.

sewer on the left bank of the Tiber was built at a great depth across the piazza Bocca della Verità. There were remains of early Republican structures nine feet below the level of the piazza, and upon them was a bed of ashes and charred materials. The buildings of a later period, above the bed of ashes, had a different orientation.

When the Emperor Nero conceived the idea of renewing and rebuilding the capital of the 'Empire, the streets were crowded with shrines, altars, and small temples which religious superstition made inviolable; his plans of improvement were opposed by the priests and by private owners of property, and any attempt to carry them out was clearly destined to lead to endless lawsuits, appraisals, and disputes among the experts. So he seems to have solved the difficulty by having the city set on fire, in the year 64 A.D. Nero was at Antium when the conflagration began, on June 18, the anniversary of the burning of Rome by the Gauls in 390 B.C. The fire started at the east end of the Circus Maximus, at the place now called La Moletta; it spread in a northeasterly direction and swept over three out of the fourteen regions of the city, partially destroying seven others. We do not possess satisfactory information in regard to all the historic monuments that perished in the flames, but we know that among them were the temple of the Moon, the foundation of which was ascribed to Servius Tullius, the Ara

Maxima, dedicated to Hercules, tradition said by Evander, the Arcadian; and the temples of Jupiter Stator, of Vesta, and of the Penates, together with the Regia. As these monuments encircled the Palatine hill, we may assume that the imperial residence on its summit was also gutted, but evidence on this point is wanting. Countless masterpieces of Greek art and many ancient relics disappeared, the loss of which the older citizens never ceased to lament, even amidst the splendour of the new city which rose from the ashes.

The charge that Nero had wilfully caused the fire is neither accepted nor rejected by Tacitus, from whom we learn that, after it had once been arrested, it burst out again in the Praedia Aemiliana, the gardens of Nero's minion, Tigellinus. Dyer suggests that the emperor merely improved the occasion to have the fire already started spread more widely and efface certain parts of the city, which he wished to rebuild. But whether the emperor was wholly or partially responsible for the conflagration, the opportunity thus afforded for rebuilding was at once improved; new plans were immediately drawn in accordance with the best engineering and architectural practice of the time. By glancing at the narrow and tortuous streets and lanes in the marble plan of the time of Septimius Severus, now in the Capitoline Museum, one may see that Nero's projects can hardly have been fully carried out; they must have left untouched the lower and more congested quarters of the city.

In May, 1877, I myself saw a strip of land which showed traces of this fearful conflagration. While the main sewer which drains the Esquiline and the region about the Coliseum was being built between the arch of Constantine and the site of the Circus Maximus, the workmen came across remains of houses, shops, and shrines on both sides of a street, neatly paved

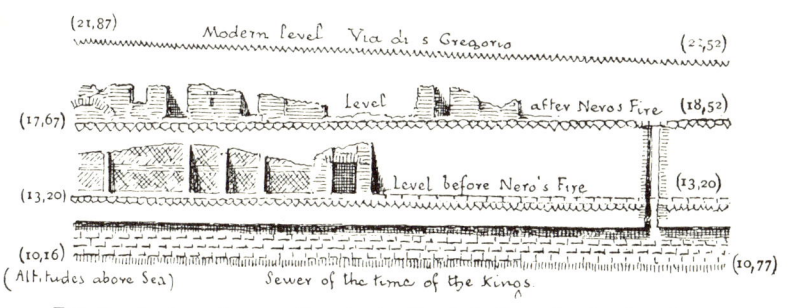

Fig. 6.—Section of excavations in the Via di S. Gregorio, showing changes of level.

with flagstones and lined by sidewalks, thirty-five feet below the present level of the ground.

The street had apparently descended from the southeast corner of the Palatine where now is the Vigna Barberini, toward the foot of the Clivus Scauri, now the Piazza di S. Gregorio. From this place, at any rate, the débris of Nero's fire were not, as might have been inferred from the statement of Tacitus,[1] carted away to the

[1] Ann. XV. 43: *Ruderi accipiendo Ostienses paludes destinabat, utique naves, quae frumentum Tiberi subvectassent, onustae rudere decurrerent.*

marshes of Ostia, but were spread on the spot; in this way the level of the valley was raised at once by ten or fifteen feet. The sectional plan presented above (Fig. 6), which I made at the time of these excavations, shows the superposition of streets and buildings before and after the fire; the altitudes are given in metres.

For the names of Nero's chief advisers and architects in the rebuilding of the city, Severus and Celer, we are indebted to Tacitus, who says of them that they were clever and daring enough to undertake, by artificial means, works the accomplishment of which nature would have denied.

A fragment of the marble mausoleum of Celer still exists in the garden of S. Agnese fuori le Mura, on the Via Nomentana (Fig. 7). The epitaph was brief but full of dignity[1]: —

CELERI · NERONIS · AVGVSTI · L[iberto] · A[rchitect]O

The block containing it was removed from the tomb by Pope Symmachus (498–514), who turned it into a capital for one of the columns of S. Agnese.

The importance of fires for the architectural history of Rome in the imperial period may easily be understood if we recall the changes caused by this means in the Forum from the time of Nero to that of Diocletian. Four times during this period the centre of Rome and

[1] Fabretti, *Inscriptiones domesticae*, p. 721, no. 431; cf. C. I. L. VI. 14,647.

of the Roman world, the CELEBERRIMVS · VRBIS · LOCVS, as it is called in an inscription,[1] was swept by flames; four times it was rebuilt on a different plan. First came the fire of Nero, just alluded to; then the fire of

FIG. 7. — Fragment of the tomb of Celer.

the reign of Titus, in 80 A.D., the damages of which were repaired by Domitian. The third occurred shortly before the death of Commodus, in 191 A.D.; the build-

[1] *Ephemeris Epigraphica*, Vol. III., 1876, p. 287.

ings were restored by Septimius Severus, his empress Julia Domna, and his son Caracalla, who shifted by thirty-three degrees the orientation of the edifices bordering on the Clivus Sacer. We have no detailed account of the conflagration in the reign of Carinus, 283 A.D., but to judge from the repairs made by Diocletian and Maxentius, affecting the Basilica Julia, the Senate-house, the Forum Julium, and the temple of Venus and Rome, it must have swept from one end of the Sacra Via to the other.

The third and last of the more important factors in the transformation and destruction of Rome under the Empire was the building of the great public baths. The thermae of Caracalla cover an area of 118,255 square metres, those of Diocletian 130,000 square metres; and the areas of both these great structures were occupied, before 212 and 305/6 A.D. respectively, by rich and populous quarters, with houses and insulae, temples, shrines, colonnades, and gardens. The buildings which stood on a higher level than that adopted for one of these bathing establishments were destroyed to the foundations; the materials of construction taken from them were saved and were made use of again in the new structure. But the buildings placed on a lower level were left standing to a height corresponding with that of the foundation of the thermae, and simply buried. This practice explains the reason why we find in some places structures of two, three, and even four different periods lying in archaeological strata one above the other.

The palace of the Flavian emperors on the Palatine rests on the remains of private houses of the end of the Republic; these, made accessible in 1721, are wrongly termed Baths of Livia. The thermae of Titus and of Trajan are built on remains of the Golden House of Nero, and this last was extended over the remains of houses built before the fire of 64 A.D.; the three strata can be easily recognised at the north entrance to the cryptoporticus of the Golden House.

The Baths of Caracalla were composed of a central building surrounded by a garden, with an outer enclosure lined with halls and rooms for bathing. Nothing is found under the built portion, because the foundations of the massive walls were of necessity carried down to the level of the virgin soil; but in the open spaces, at a depth of only a few inches below the surface, are found remains of extensive houses and other buildings which Caracalla purchased and covered up.[1]

When the Via Nazionale, the main thoroughfare of modern Rome, was cut in 1877 across the ridge of the Quirinal, — then occupied by the Aldobrandini and Rospigliosi gardens, — the workmen first brought to light remains of the thermae of Constantine; underneath

[1] A part of one of these houses, excavated in 1860–1867 by Guidi, is shown in *Ruins and Excavations*, Fig. 39.

these were remains of the house of Claudius Claudianus and of another once belonging to Avidius Quietus; and lastly, on a lower level, were walls of early reticulate work (Fig. 8).

Subsequent excavations on the site of the same baths have given us the means of reconstructing the map of this part of the Quirinal prior to the time of Constantine, and of obtaining a list, possibly complete, of the public and private buildings purchased and demolished by this Emperor in or about 315 A.D. The list comprises the palaces of T. Flavius Claudius Claudianus and of T. Avidius Quietus already mentioned; the palace and gardens of a C. Art(orius?) Germanianus, of a Claudia Vera, of a Lucius Naevius Clemens, of a Marcus Postumius Festus; and a sacred edifice, the roof of which was made of marble tiles. These tiles Constantine's architect made use of in laying the foundations of the Caldarium, from which we dug them out, one by one, in 1879. They were all marked with a number, so that, in making repairs, the roof could be taken off and put together again without difficulty by observing the sequence of the figures. In another part of the same foundations we found many fragments of statues and sculptured marbles built, as common materials, into the rubble work.

A similar statement would hold good for the Baths of Diocletian. The excavations made within the limits of this immense structure since 1870 in connexion

FIG. 8. — Excavation of the Via Nazionale on the Quirinal, showing remains of buildings of different periods.

with work on the railway station, the Piazza dei Cinquecento, the Grand Hotel, and the Massimi palace, as well as the cutting of streets and the laying out of new gardens, have brought to light the remains of several preëxisting edifices, — among them the offices of a Collegium Fortunae Felicis, and a temple built on foundations of concrete; a colonnade or shrine rebuilt by Gnaeus Sentius Saturninus; pavements of streets, walls of private houses, and a reservoir. The materials of all these buildings, brick and marble, were used over again in the foundations of the baths.

CHAPTER III

THE USE OF EARLIER MATERIALS, PARTICULARLY MARBLES, IN THE BUILDING OPERATIONS OF THE LATER EMPIRE

THE practice of building walls with architectural marbles, blocks containing inscriptions, statues, and other fine materials from previous structures, goes at least as far back as the reign of Septimius Severus (193-211 A.D.). The propylaea of the Porticus Octaviae were restored by him, in the year 203, with sculptured fragments from edifices damaged or ruined by the fire of Titus. The upper story of the Coliseum was likewise restored by Severus Alexander in 223, and by Traianus Decius in 250, with a patchwork of stones of every description, — trunks of columns, fragments of entablatures, lintels and doorposts taken from the amphitheatre itself, which had been damaged by fire, or brought from other buildings; several of the fragments can be recognised in the accompanying illustrations (Figs. 9, 10).

Another instance of certain date is that of a private bathing establishment discovered January 30, 1873, at the junction of the Via Ariosto with the Piazza Dante

USE OF EARLIER MATERIALS

on the Esquiline. It was a graceful little building, dating from the time of Diocletian and Constantine, as proved by hundreds of brick stamps of that period found in the walls above ground. The walls below the

FIG. 9. — Part of the upper story of the Coliseum, repaired with materials from earlier buildings.

surface were built of statues and miscellaneous fragments of marble. There were life-size or semi-colossal figures of Minerva, of the Indian Bacchus and of Aesculapius, besides several torsos and other fragments of considerable value; a column shaped like the lictor's fasces, with capital and base; and the basin of a fountain in pure Greek style.[1]

A more familiar illustration is the triumphal arch of Constantine, erected by the Meta Sudans in 315 A.D. This monument, so compact and perfect to the eye, is

FIG. 10. — Another view of the upper story of the Coliseum, showing repairs made with architectural fragments from various sources.

really a striking example of the way in which old structures were pillaged to erect new ones. If we climb to the chamber above the arch (there is a nar-

[1] *Bull. Com.*, 1875, p. 79, Tav. XI. Fig. 1, 2; Helbig, *Guide to the Public Collections of Classical Antiquities in Rome*, Vol. I. p. 444, no. 601.

row staircase in the side facing the Palatine), we shall see why Milizia gave it the nickname of Cornacchia di Esopo, "Aesop's crow." We shall find that the bas-reliefs of the attic, the statues of the Dacian kings, the eight medallions above the side passages, the eight columns of giallo antico, and the greater part of the entablature were removed from a triump'.al arch of Trajan, probably the *arcus divi Traiani* which spanned the Via Appia (or the Via Nova) near the Porta Capena. The inside of the structure also is built with a great variety of materials taken from the tombs of the Fabii and of the Arruntii, the carvings and inscriptions of which are still perfect.

Under the rule of Constantine, the dismantling of earlier buildings for the sake of their materials became a common practice; this statement, startling as it may appear, will not be considered extravagant by any one who has read Ciampini's "De sacris aedificiis a Constantino magno constructis,"[1] or Marangoni's "Delle cose gentilesche e profane trasportate ad uso delle chiese,"[2] or Grimaldi's "Diary of the Destruction of Old St. Peter's."[3]

After the defeat of Maxentius, in the year 312, Constantine "erected a basilica over the tomb of the blessed Peter."[4] This was built hurriedly, and in its

[1] Romae, per I. Jacobum Komarck, 1693, in fol.
[2] Romae, 1744, in 4°.   [3] Cod. Barberin, XXXIV. 50.
[4] *Liber Pontificalis*, Sylvester, XVI. p. 176.

construction first of all a part of the adjoining circus of Caligula and Nero was utilised. The left wing of the sacred edifice was carried over the three northern walls of the circus, which had supported the seats of the spectators on the side of the Via Cornelia. The columns for the basilica were brought together from all quarters. In one of the note-books of Antonio da Sangallo the younger,[1] I found a memorandum of the quality, size, colour, and other details in regard to one hundred and thirty-six shafts. Nearly all the ancient quarries were represented in the collection, not to speak of styles and periods. Grimaldi says that he could not find two capitals or two bases alike. He adds that the architrave and frieze differed from one intercolumniation to another, and that some of the blocks bore inscriptions with the names and praises of Titus, Trajan, Gallienus, and others. The walls of the basilica, except the apse and the arches, were patched with fragments of tiles and of stone. On each side of the first entrance, at the foot of the steps, were two granite columns, with composite capitals showing the bust of the Emperor Hadrian framed in acanthus leaves.

In the construction of all the Christian buildings of the fourth century we may well believe that there was a similar indebtedness to pagan sources. Some of these edifices, as the church of S. Agnese and the adjoining mausoleum of Constantia on the Via Nomentana,

[1] These note-books are now in the Uffizi, Florence.

the church of St. Lawrence on the Via Tiburtina, and the church of S. Clemente, are still standing within or without the walls. Additional proof may be found in the accounts left by those who saw the Basilica Salvatoris in Laterano, and that of St. Paul on the road to Ostia, before their modernisation. In some instances the location and use of blocks of marble have been changed three or four times. A pedestal of a statue erected in the year 193 in the town hall of some municipality in the vicinity of Rome, was utilised in the restoration of the Baths of Caracalla in 285. Rufius Volusianus, prefect of the City in 365, removed the block from the Baths and turned it into a monument in honour of Valentinian I. It seems finally to have disappeared about 1548 in a lime-kiln of Pope Paul III.[1]

The great department of imperial administration called "Department of Marbles" (*statio marmorum*), apparently suspended operations before the middle of the fourth century; at any rate we have been unable to find any structure built after the time of Constantine with materials fresh from the quarry. This is the more remarkable in view of the fact that on the banks of the Tiber at the marble wharves (La Marmorata) and on those of Trajan's channel (Canale di Fiumicino), where the marbles belonging to the Emperor or to private importers were landed, there still remained a vast number of unused blocks. These two sources of supply have

[1] *C. I. L.* VI. 1173.

been drawn upon by means of excavations almost uninterruptedly since the time of the Cosmatis, and yet their wealth in blocks and columns of the rarest kinds of breccias seems hardly to have diminished. The Romans of the fourth century, however, emperors as well as private citizens, thought it less troublesome to rob the splendid monuments of the Republic and early Empire of their ornaments already carved, and to transfer these to their own clumsy structures, than to work anew the materials stored at La Marmorata. Abundant evidence on this point may be gained, not merely from ecclesiastical, but also from secular structures, as the four-faced arch of the Forum Boarium, the temple of Saturn on the Clivus Capitolinus, the bridges of Cestius (S. Bartolomeo) and of Valentinian (Ponte Sisto), the Grain Exchange at the church of S. Maria in Cosmedin, the arena and podium of the Coliseum, the Porticus Maximae of Gratian, the monumental columns on the Sacra Via, the market-hall of the Caelian (S. Stefano Rotondo), the market-place of the Esquiline near S. Vito, the shops at the east of the Forum Romanum, and a hundred other buildings of the Decadence.

There are on record several edicts of Constantius II. (350–361) having to do with the compulsory closing of heathen temples. According to Libanius he often made a present of a temple, just as one might give away a dog or a horse; and Ammianus makes mention of some courtiers who had received gifts of this kind.[1] But the fate of pagan edifices and their precious works of art was sealed in the year 383, when Gratian did away with all the privileges of the temples and priests, and confiscated their revenues. Eight years later Valentinian and Theodosius prohibited sacrifices, even if strictly domestic and private.

These decisive measures led to open rebellion on the part of those who still clung to the ancient beliefs, but after the defeat of the rebel leader Eugenius, which took place early in September, 394, the temples were closed forever. Strange to say, this prohibition of the pagan worship contributed for the time being to the embellishment of certain parts of the City, such as the forums, the baths, and the courts of justice, where the statues of the gods, expelled from their august seats, were set up and exhibited simply as works of art.[2] This is referred to in the words which Prudentius puts into the mouth of Theodosius, when addressing the Senate after the defeat of Eugenius (*Contra Sym.* I. 501-505): —

> Marmora tabenti respergine tincta lavate,
> O proceres, liceat statuas consistere puras
> Artificum magnorum opera: haec pulcherrima nostrae
> Ornamenta fuant patriae nec decolor usus
> In vitium versae monumenta coinquinet artis.

[1] See Dyer, *History of the City of Rome*, ed. of 1865, p. 308.

[2] Interesting information on this subject will be found in *C. I. L.* Vol. VI. Part I.; see also de Rossi's papers in *Bull. di archeologia cristiana*, 1865, p. 5, and *Bull. Com.*, 1874, p. 174.

The practice of removing statuary from places of worship to civil edifices is, however, older by half a century than the decree of 394. As early as the year 331 Anicius Paulinus, prefect of the City, transferred statues to the thermae of the Decii on the Aventine (*C. I. L.* VI. 1651); Fabius Titianus lined the Sacra Via with other examples of the sculptor's art in 339–341; in the same way Fabius Felix Passifilus Paulinus embellished the Baths of Titus in 355, Clodius Hermogenianus the Baths of Trajan in 368–370. The Basilica Julia was likewise ornamented with borrowed statues by Gabinius Vettius Probianus in 377; parts of the pedestals on which five of them stood have come to light (*C. I. L.* VI. 1658), and contain inscriptions with the formula, *statuam quae basilicae Juliae a se noviter reparatae ornamento esset, adiecit.* Some of these masterpieces were of Greek origin; one was attributed to Praxiteles, the others to Polyclitus, Timarchus, and Bryaxis.

From inscriptions we learn also that in later times statues were overthrown by the barbarians in their incursions, and by the citizens in civil strifes. A pedestal discovered in the fifteenth century near S. Maria Nuova, at the top of the Clivus Sacer, bore the inscription: *Castalius Innocentius Audax v(ir) c(larissimus) praef(ectus) urbis* . . . . *barbarica incursione sublata restituit* (*C. I. L.* VI. 1663). Another, discovered during the pontificate of Julius III. (1550–1555), speaks of a statue of Minerva that had been thrown down at the time of a fire caused by a riot, and set up again by Anicius Acilius Aginatius, apparently in 483 A.D. (*C. I. L.* VI. 1664).

To what use the temples were put immediately after the expulsion of their gods, we do not know; but it is certain that they were not occupied by Christians, nor turned into places of Christian worship. This change was only to take place two centuries later, when the scruples about the propriety of worshipping the true God in heathen temples had been overcome.

In the year 609, Pope Boniface IV. "asked the Emperor Phocas for the temple which was called Pantheon, and turned it into a church of Mary the Virgin ever blessed." Two periods, then, may be distinguished in the converting of pagan edifices into places of Christian worship, one anterior to the year 609, the other following that date. During the first, civil edifices alone were transformed, partially or completely, into churches; such were the Record Office, which became the church of SS. Cosmas and Damian, and the round market on the Caelian Hill, now S. Stefano Rotondo. After 609 almost every available building, whether secular or sacred, was made into a church or chapel, until the places of worship seemed to outnumber the houses.

We must not imagine, however, that the good-will of the emperors and the guardianship of the prefects of the City saved all statues from destruction. Far from it! Public protection was extended only to the works of art which adorned the streets, squares, baths, parks, and public buildings, few in number when compared with the thousands upon thousands that belonged to private owners. A special magistrate was appointed to take charge of this branch of public administration, under the title of *Curator Statuarum*, "Keeper of Statues"; but the office was not long kept up. King Theoderic and his adviser Cassiodorius revived it in the year 500, in order to save the statues from the hands of lime-burners, stone-cutters, and masons, the three bodies of marble-hunters mentioned by Cassiodorius (*Variar.* VII. 13). The Curator Statuarum then had the help of two assessors, — one to protect the abandoned buildings from illegal plundering, the other to control the lime-kilns; and yet Theoderic himself caused the columns and marbles of the Domus Pinciana to be removed from Rome to Ravenna.[1]

The destruction of marble statuary may well be illustrated by the fate of the *pretiosissima deorum simulacra*, "most precious images of the gods," placed by Augustus in the compital shrines at the crossings of the main thoroughfares of the City, in the years 10–7 B.C. The number of these shrines — about two hundred in the time of Augustus — had been increased to two hundred and sixty-five in 73 A.D., and to

[1] Cassiod. *Variar.* III. 10, ed. Mommsen.

three hundred and twenty-four at the beginning of the fourth century. They offered an almost complete chronological series of works of Greek plastic art to the appreciation of the citizens of Rome. What has become of all these "most precious images"? If we consider that only one plinth and four pedestals[1] of that incomparable series have come down to us, we cannot doubt that the three hundred and twenty-four "most precious images" of Greek workmanship belonging to the compital shrines shared the same fate as those from the temples, — they were broken to pieces, and the pieces thrown into the lime-kilns, or built into the walls of new buildings, as if they were the cheapest rubble.

Foundation walls built up in part of statues and busts have been found by the score. I add here a few examples from the "Memoirs" of Flaminio Vacca (1594) and of Pietro Sante Bartoli (about 1675).[2]

"A foundation wall which runs under the hospital of St. John Lateran," Vacca reports, "is built entirely of fragments of excellent statuary. I saw there knees and

---

[1] The plinth was discovered in 1896, near the so-called temple of Mater Matuta (S. Maria del Sole) in the piazza Bocca della Verità. It belonged to a celebrated work of Scopas the younger, being inscribed OPVS SCOPAE MINORIS, — a statue of Hercules, surnamed Olivarius from the location of the shrine near the Olive Market. See Huelsen, "Il Foro Boario," in *Dissert. Accad. archeol.* Serie II. Vol. VI. p. 261. I have described the four pedestals in *Pagan and Christian Rome*, pp. 34, 35.

[2] Edited by Fea in Vol. I. of the *Miscellanea*, Rome, 1790.

elbows modelled in the style of the Laocoon of the Belvedere" (*Mem.* p. 13). Further, "In the walls and foundations of an old house, which stood near S. Lorenzo fuori le Mura, and was pulled down to make room for a square in front of that church, eighteen or twenty portrait-busts of emperors were discovered. Most of them were removed to the Farnese Gallery" (*ibid.* p. 14). And again, "A great block of masonry was levelled to the ground in the vineyard of Hannibal Caro, outside the Porta San Giovanni, for the improvement of the plantation. A complete set of busts of the twelve Caesars, as well as of other emperors, a marble sarcophagus bearing bas-reliefs of the twelve labours of Hercules, and other fine marbles were found embedded in the masonry. I have forgotten what became of the busts; the front of the sarcophagus, however, was cut away and sent to Nuvolara, a villa of Monsignor Visconti," on the left bank of the Po (*ibid.* p. 48).

"When the Via Graziosa was opened in 1684," says Bartoli, "along the north slope of the Cespian, opposite S. Lorenzo in Panisperna, remains of ancient houses were found,[1] and fragments of an exquisite statue of Venus built into a wall. The statue was afterwards restored by Ercole Ferrata for Queen Christine of Sweden" (*Mem.* p. 17). Finally, "In exploring the cellar of a house on the Corso, the famous architect,

[1] See *Ruins and Excavations*, p. 393, Fig. 149.

Lorenzo Bernini, discovered seven statues broken in pieces and built into a wall. The statues were restored almost perfectly, so few were the fragments missing" (*ibid.* p. 42).

Francesco de' Ficoroni saw, in the year 1693, "a very great number of fragments of the most beautiful statues, which had served as building materials" for the foundations of the Torre di Nona, near the bridge of S. Angelo (*Mem.* p. 2). The same archaeologist speaks of blocks of alabaster discovered, in 1705, under the last tower of the City walls on the left bank of the Tiber, by the Monte Testaccio. One of the blocks of alabastro fiorito was cut into slabs and used in the decoration of the front of the altar of the Madonna del Sasso in the Pantheon (*ibid.* p. 105). A replica of the Laocoon is known to be buried in the substructures of the church of S. Pudentiana, and a fine statue of colossal size under S. Marcello.

Were I to relate my personal experience in the way of similar finds, the entire volume would hardly suffice for the narrative. In all sorts of places, both within and without the walls of the City, I have come across fragments of statuary used as rubble, in the older strata as well as in those of later periods. Two or three instances must answer for all.

Toward the end of the second or the beginning of the third century, a colony of Greek sculptors came to Rome from Aphrodisias, in Caria, and set up a studio on the Esquiline hill, between the Baths of Titus and the gardens of Maecenas. They were active artists indeed, and worked harmoniously under the mastership of a leader, whom they called ἀρχιερεύς (high priest). One day their workshop and their exhibition rooms came to grief; whether by fire, or by the fall of the building, or by violence of men, I cannot tell. In the spring of 1886, when the Via Buonarroti was being cut through in the direction of the Baths of Titus, a wall was discovered entirely built with the contents of the studio. There were statues of Jupiter, Juno, Pluto, Aesculapius, Cybele, Minerva Parthenos, Hercules; bacchic vases, fountains, mouths of wells, candelabras, figures of animals, bas-reliefs, and other carvings; and nearly all the works were signed by one of the members of this artistic brotherhood from Aphrodisias — seventeen signatures in all. The fact that no essential portions of each work were missing shows that they were brought entire to the scene of destruction, and then broken up and thrown into a foundation wall.

Two years and a half later, in November, 1888, a discovery of the same kind was made on the site of the temple of Isis, now crossed by the Via Michelangelo, the Via Galileo, Via Leopardi, and other streets. Another wall was found containing three or four hundred fragments of sculpture, out of which fourteen statues, or important portions of statues, have been reconstructed. They represent Jupiter, Serapis, Isis crowned with poppies and ears of grain, and the same goddess veiled, with a crescent on her forehead ; there are also three replicas of the same type, and a female figure wearing the Egyptian head-dress, probably a portrait-statue. These marbles are, beyond doubt, spoils from the great temple close by, hammered and broken and utilised as building materials, after the closing of the temple itself. Apparently the sanctuary supplied marbles and stone to the whole neighbourhood for centuries. At the foot of the platform on which it stood another wall was found in December, 1888, built with blocks of amethyst breccia (*breccia ametistina*), amounting in all to twenty or twenty-five cubic feet.

In 1884, while collecting specimens of rare marbles, to be exhibited in the Museo Urbano in the Orto Botanico, I was shown a beautiful piece of purplish granite, with oval spots resembling in shape and colour those of a leopard's skin, which had just been discovered under the Hickson Field palace, on the Via Merulana. As the block was not entirely shapeless, but bore marks of the chisel on one side, it was given to me with the stipulation that if, in the future, other pieces of the same object should be found, the donation should be cancelled. Two years later, when the convent of the Cluny Sisters was being built, at a distance of six hundred feet from the Field palace, what should be brought to light but the missing portions of that very work of art ! It was a beautiful and nearly perfect replica of the sacred cow, Hathor, — the symbol of Isis, — seemingly copied from the original, discovered in 1884 among the ruins of the temple of Isis in the Campus Martius. After such instances of the destruction and dispersion of statuary, can we wonder at the fate of

FIG. 11. — A statue, broken into fragments, in process of reconstruction.

the Farnese Hercules, the torso of which was found in the Baths of Caracalla, the head at the bottom of a well in the Trastevere, and the legs at Bovillae, ten miles from Rome?

USE OF EARLIER MATERIALS

In the accompanying illustration (Fig. 11) we see in process of reconstruction a statue of Victory that had been broken into 151 pieces. It was discovered in the house of L. Aurelius Avianius Symmachus on the Caelian.[1]

My experience in the excavations at Rome has suggested the following observation in regard to the condition of marble statues when discovered: Those found in loose earth, among the ruins of the edifices to which they belonged, generally lack head and arms; but those that have been used as building material in foundation walls can often be reconstructed in their entirety, head and arms being not far away.

These facts show that before the burial of Ancient Rome, many of the statues had been injured by knocking off their most prominent and easily broken parts. The loss of head and arms may in some cases have resulted from the overthrowing of the statue, the body remaining where it fell, the head rolling off to one side. Most of the loose heads are rounded and smooth as if street-idlers had used them to play the popular game of *bocce*.[2] Some of them have a hook or ring on the crown, and must have been used as weights for large

[1] *Ruins and Excavations*, p. 347.

[2] This is a purely Italian game played with six larger balls and one smaller one, which is used as a mark. Each of the two players rolls three balls, and those that stop nearest the mark gain a point. The temptation to use loose heads of statues when wooden balls were not available must have been strong.

scales. The five or six hundred heads discovered in my time were all, except a dozen or two, without noses. The fact that heads and arms of statues used as building materials are rarely missing, shows that the breaking up of statuary became common at a comparatively early period of the Roman decadence, when the works of art ornamenting palaces and gardens had as yet suffered but little injury.

CHAPTER IV

THE ASPECT OF THE CITY AT THE BEGINNING OF THE FIFTH CENTURY

ALTHOUGH Rome had not recovered, and could not recover, from the removal of the imperial court to Byzantium, accomplished in 330, yet at the beginning of the fifth century the great buildings still remained substantially intact, and a few additions were made to the list of existing monuments. The architectural impressiveness of the City may be measured by the effect that it produced upon the mind of Constantius II., who visited it in 357, twenty-seven years after the Palatine had ceased to be the seat of imperial government. A graphic account of the visit is given by Ammianus Marcellinus in the tenth chapter of Book XVI., from which I quote but one passage referring to the Forum of Trajan: —

" Having now entered the Forum Trajanum, the most marvellous creation of human genius, he was struck with wonder, and looked around in amazement at the great structures, which no pen can describe, and which mankind can create and behold but once in the course of centuries. . . . Then he turned his attention to the equestrian statue in the centre of the Forum, and said to his attendants he would have one like it in Constantinople: to which Hormisdas, a young Persian prince attached to the court, replied, 'You must first provide your horse with a stable like this.'"

Constantius was indeed overwhelmed by the greatness of Rome. The other edifices mentioned as having especially astonished him are the temple of Jupiter on the Capitoline, the Baths, the Flavian Amphitheatre, the Pantheon, the temple of Venus and Rome, the theatre of Pompey, the Odeum, and the Stadium.

There is also a monumental record of this imperial visit: the highest obelisk of the world, erected by Thothmes III. before the great temple at Thebes, removed by Constantius to Rome, and set up in the Circus Maximus. It now stands in the piazza of the Lateran. Constantius is said to have taken away the superb statue of Victory, presented by Augustus, from the Senate-house; but it must have been saved from injury, for Julian the Apostate (361–363) was able to place it again on its pedestal.

It is difficult for us to form a conception of the magnificence of Rome, even in its decline. According to the regionary catalogue compiled in the time of Constantine,[1] the City then "contained 2 circuses, 2 amphi-

---

[1] There are two editions of this catalogue. The first, known by the name of *Notitia Regionum Urbis Romae*, dates from A.D. 334; the second, called *Curiosum urbis Romae regionum XIV.*, must have been

theatres, 3 theatres, 10 basilicas, 11 thermae, 36 arches of marble, 2 commemorative columns, 6 obelisks (imported from Egypt), 423 temples, 1790 *domus*—that is, extensive private residences, or palaces, of the wealthy —besides which there were reckoned 46,602 tenements (*insulae*). The open places were adorned with 2 *colossi* (probably those of Nero and Augustus), 22 'great horses'—presumably counting not merely the large equestrian statues, as that of Marcus Aurelius, now in the square of the Capitol, but also groups of which horses formed a part, as those of the Dioscuri on the Capitoline and of the Horse-tamers on the Quirinal; to which are added 80 gilded and 77 ivory statues of the gods, no mention being made of the countless lesser statues on every side." In the number of obelisks, at any rate, the catalogue falls far short of the truth; and statistics such as these, impressive though they may be, are after all of no real assistance in trying to form an idea of the aspect of the City unless we are able to reconstruct, in imagination, the buildings and works of art so concisely summarised.

The year 403 is memorable for the celebration of a triumph, the last ever seen in Ancient Rome. A century had elapsed since the Romans had beheld such a

issued in or after 357, because it mentions the obelisk raised in that year in the Circus Maximus. For a bibliography on these two invaluable documents see *Ruins and Excavations*, p. vii.

sight — Diocletian's triumph in 303; nay, in that space of time they had only thrice seen the face of an emperor. The pretext for this pageant was the subjugation of the Numidian rebel, Count Gildo. This event is commemorated by several existing monuments. One is a pedestal of an equestrian group, discovered in the Forum near the arch of Septimius Severus between 1549 and 1565; it bears an inscription, from which we learn that it was erected by the Senate and the Roman people as a testimonial of their rejoicing at the crushing of the rebellion and the recovery of Africa. In the same place was found the pedestal of a statue erected in honour of Stilicho, the inscription of which distinctly attributes to him the reconquest of Africa, directly in the face of the historical evidence.[1] A third inscription, commemorating the repairing of the Claudian and Marcian aqueducts, in the plain of Arsoli, with the money confiscated from the rebels, is preserved in the palace of Prince Massimi at Arsoli.

Another historic monument relating to the Gothic wars stands on the edge of the Forum opposite the Senate-house. The inscription praises the gallantry of the army of Arcadius, Honorius, and Theodosius in defeating Rhadagaisus at the battle of Florence in 405; the victory being attributed to Stilicho, — *post con-*

[1] See Huelsen, "*Il monumento della guerra Gildonica sul Foro Romano,*" in *Mittheil.*, 1895, p. 52; *C. I. L.* VI. 1187, 1730.

fectum Gothicum bellum . . . consiliis et fortitudine . . . Flavii Stilichonis.[1]

FIG. 12. — The monument of Stilicho in the Forum.

This memorial, shown in our illustration (Fig. 12), set up "by decree of the Senate and the Roman people,

[1] *Notizie degli Scavi*, 1880, p. 53.

under the care of Pisidius Romulus, prefect of the City," is the meanest and poorest in the whole Forum. It presents indisputable evidence of the decline of pride, taste, and resources at the beginning of the fifth century. It is made of two blocks, one of travertine, which forms the base, and one of marble above. The marble block had previously been used as a pedestal for an equestrian statue of bronze; the statue was knocked off, the pedestal set up awkwardly on one end, the cracks in it being brought together with iron clamps; then the old inscription was carefully obliterated, and the new one cut over it. In the same year, 405, a triumphal arch was raised to the three Emperors — with spoils of other edifices — "because they had swept from the face of the earth the nation of the Goths." Four years later, the very barbarians whom they boasted to have annihilated, stormed and sacked the city.

The arch just mentioned stood by the church of S. Orso, near S. Giovanni de' Fiorentini. Just as in classical times, such honorary monuments were raised on the Sacra Via, leading to the great temple of Jupiter Optimus Maximus, so now, in the Christian era, they were built over the roads converging towards St. Peter's, and especially at the foot of the bridges which the pilgrims had to cross on their way to the Apostle's tomb. The arch of Gratianus, Valentinianus, and Theodosius, erected in the year 382, stood in the

Piazza di Ponte S. Angelo, that of Arcadius, Honorius, and Theodosius (405 A.D.) at the approach to the Pons Vaticanus, that of Valentinian and Valens (366–367) by the Ponte Sisto.

The Emperors Arcadius and Honorius, fearing an advance of the Goths under Alaric, undertook the general restoration of the City walls under the direction of Stilicho. The work was finished in January, 402, and celebrated by several inscriptions, three of which, cut on the Porta Tiburtina, Porta Praenestina, and Porta Portuensis, have come down to us.[1] They speak not only of "the restoration of the walls, gates, and towers of the Eternal City," but also of "the removal of large masses of rubbish." This allusion to the disposition of rubbish is of great importance for our subject, because it gives us the date and the cause of the first great rise in the level of the City, at least of the outlying districts. After the removal of the imperial court to Byzantium, the municipal regulations requiring the removal of the City refuse to a safe distance apparently fell into abeyance; and all sorts of material seem to have been heaped up against the walls. Stilicho had neither time nor means to cart away the bank of débris, which certainly diminished his chances of a successful defence; so he contented himself with levelling it off and spreading it over the adjoining land. In 402, therefore, the level of imperial Rome on the

[1] *C. I. L.* VI. 1188–1190.

line of the walls was raised at once by ten or twelve feet.

The best evidence of this fact is to be found at the Porta Ostiensis, now Porta di S. Paolo, close to the pyramid of Cestius (Fig. 13). The threshold of the gate of 402 is about twelve feet higher than the base of the pyramid and the threshold of the gate of 272. Again, the arch of Augustus on the Via Tiburtina, which

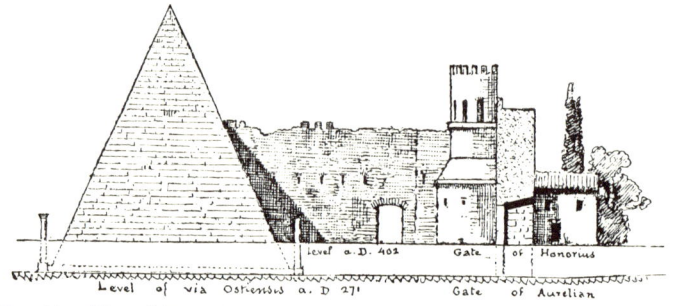

Fig. 13. — The raising of level at the Porta Ostiensis, A.D. 402. The Pyramid of Cestius is shown at the left.

formed the Tiburtine gate of 272, is ten or twelve feet lower than the gate of 402.[1] The same observation applies to the Porta Flaminia, Porta Praenestina, Porta Portuensis, and Porta Septimiana. The Porta Appia seems to have been rebuilt with materials taken from the beautiful temple of Mars outside the walls, without any change of level. In only one part of the walls have I found traces of a lowering of the soil below the

[1] See the illustration in *Ruins and Excavations*, p. 76.

level of the classical period. This single exception is at the northeast corner of the Praetorian camp.

The gates of Honorius have been ruthlessly treated in modern times. Sixtus IV. dismantled the Porta Flaminia in 1478; Alexander VI. destroyed the Porta Septimiana in 1498; Pius IV., the Nomentana in 1564; Urban VIII., the Portuensis and the Aurelia in 1642; Gregory XVI., the Praenestina in 1838. In 1869 Pius IX. dismantled the Porta Tiburtina, in order to make use of the stones of which it was built in the foundations of the "Colonna del Concilio" at the church of S. Pietro in Montorio. The Porta Salaria, damaged in the bombardment of September 20, 1870, was rebuilt in its present form in 1872.

CHAPTER V

THE SACK OF THE GOTHS IN 410, AND ITS CONSEQUENCES

THE repairing of the city walls by Arcadius and Honorius was accomplished none too soon. The success of Stilicho in checking the advance of the Goths at the battle of Florence, in 405, was only temporary; the barbarian host, two hundred thousand strong, had overrun the plains of northern Italy, and would undoubtedly take advantage of a favourable opportunity to attack Rome itself. Such an opportunity came with the disgrace and death of Stilicho, who was banished in 407 and murdered at Ravenna in 408; his name was even erased from the monument erected in his honour in the Forum, described in the previous chapter. The Roman leader had hardly been put out of the way before Rome saw, for the first time since the Gallic invasion of 390 B.C., a host of barbarians surrounding the walls. This time Alaric was induced to lead his army away by the payment of an exorbitant ransom, one of the items of which was five thousand pounds of gold. In order to meet this demand, the Romans were compelled to strip the bronze statues of their heavy gilding.[1]

Two years later, in 410, Alaric and his hordes entered the City, on the twenty-fourth day of August, in the dead of night by the Porta Salaria, and set fire to the houses near the gate, among which was the imperial mansion in the gardens of Sallust. The lives of the citizens were spared, but the City was abandoned to plunder, except as regards the two sacred enclosures of St. Peter and St. Paul. At the end of the third day the barbarians withdrew, carrying off an incredible amount of articles of value, among which — if we are to believe Procopius — were the spoils of the temple at Jerusalem which Titus had placed in the temple of Peace; but the testimony of Procopius on this point may well be doubted.

In these days of terror the Aventine with its 130 palaces, the most aristocratic quarter of the city, suffered more than all the other regions. I have witnessed excavations made in the Vigna Torlonia, among the remains of the Thermae Decianae and of the house of Trajan; in the Vigna Maciocchi, among the ruins of the palace of Annia Cornificia Faustina, younger sister of Marcus Aurelius and wife of Ummidius Quadratus; in the garden of S. Anselmo, where the palace of the

[1] Zosimus, V. 45, speaks of the actual melting of gold and silver statues, and also of the gold and silver ornaments of bronze or marble statues.

Pactumeii was discovered in 1892; and in the garden of S. Sabina, once occupied by the houses of Cosmus, Minister of Finance under Marcus Aurelius, and of Marcella and Principia, the friends of St. Jerome. In watching these excavations, I was struck by the fact that these beautiful palaces must have perished towards the beginning of the fifth century of our era, and all from the same cause. The signs of destruction are everywhere the same: traces of flames which blackened the red ground of the frescoes, and caused the roofs to fall on the mosaic or marble pavements of the ground floor; coins scattered among the ruins, belonging, with rare exceptions, to the fourth century; statues that had been restored over and over again; marbles stolen from pagan buildings, mostly from sepulchral monuments, and utilised for hurried restorations; and Christian symbols on lamps and domestic utensils. These indications fix the period and point to the same historical event, — the capture and pillage of Rome by the Goths in August, 410. The Aventine paid dearly for the partiality shown for it by the noble and the wealthy. The treasures accumulated in its palaces roused the cupidity of the invaders, and led them to excesses of plunder and destruction such as were spared to more humble districts of the City.

Although the imperial casino in the gardens of Sallust is the only structure distinctly mentioned by historians as having been consumed by fire, we are constantly discovering evidences of a far more widespread loss from this cause; and even among the written records of those eventful days some new particulars come to light, from time to time, as in the following instance: —

On the Caelian Hill, between S. Stefano Rotondo and the Lateran, there was a palace belonging to the descendants of the Valerii Poplicolae, namely, to Valerius Severus, prefect of Rome in the year 386, and to his son Pinianus, husband of Melania the younger. The palace was so beautiful and contained so much wealth, that when Pinianus and Melania, crushed with grief on account of the loss of all their children, put it up for sale in 404, they found none willing to purchase it — *ad tam magnum et mirabile opus accedere nemo ausus fuit.* However, seven or eight years later the same palace was sold for little or nothing — *domus pro nihilo venumdata est.* The reason for such a change has lately been discovered in a manuscript of the library of Chartres. The barbarians had plundered the palace of all its valuables, and wrecked it by fire.[1]

Additional evidence regarding the fate of the palaces on the Aventine is furnished by St. Jerome, in Epistles 54 and 127. One of these palaces, as we have seen, belonged to Marcella, the founder of monastic life in Rome. This noble matron was left a widow after seven months of marriage, and being pressed by the Consul Cerealis to marry again, determined to sever

[1] Compare, however, *Ruins and Excavations,* p. 345.

all connection with the world for the rest of her life. Following the rule of St. Athanasius, Bishop of Alexandria, she dressed herself in simple garb, gave up the use of wine and meat, and divided her time between the study of the Scriptures, prayers, and pilgrimages to the tombs of apostles and martyrs. St. Jerome became Marcella's spiritual adviser; such was the serenity and beauty of her character, that in one of his letters she is addressed as "the pride of Roman matrons." However, when Rome became the prey of the Goths, the barbarians broke into her peaceful retreat and tortured her in an attempt to discover the secret hiding-place of her treasures, treasures that she had long before given up to the needy. Fearing more for the safety of Principia, whom she had adopted as a spiritual daughter, than for her own life, she threw herself at the feet of the Gothic chieftain and begged to be conducted to the church of St. Paul outside the walls, which, like St. Peter's, had been set apart by Alaric as a refuge for women and children. The destruction of her Aventine home and the shock of the torture and pillage brought Marcella's life to a close; she died before the end of that eventful August.

The barbarians attacked with equal fury the public buildings of the Aventine, especially the thermae. One of these establishments, called Thermae Decianae from the family of the Caecinae Decii, who had built it in the neighbourhood of their palace, was undermined by the Goths so that the main wall of the tepidarium leaned forward, dragging into its own ruin all the neighbouring halls. The damages, as well as the repairs made in haste by Caecina Decius Albinus in the year 414, are described in an inscription discovered on the spot in 1725, and now preserved in the Capitoline Museum.[1] The temple of Juno Regina, first erected by Camillus after the capture of Veii, and rebuilt in imperial times with great magnificence, seems to have been seriously injured, if not destroyed, on this occasion. Its marbles were made use of by Peter, an Illyrian priest, who built the church of S. Sabina in 425.

Such being the fate of the Aventine, with its luxurious homes and countless treasures, it need not surprise us if the Genius of the place (as the ancients would say) has now and then vouchsafed to us modern searchers after antiquities a truly remarkable find. Such a find was that made in the pontificate of Pius IV. by Matteo da Castello, the Pope's architect, who, while planting a vineyard near the church of S. Prisca, came across two or three receptacles of lead, containing eighteen hundred pieces of gold, with the image of the Empress Helena on one side, and the symbol of the cross on the other. He duly notified the Pope of his discovery, and received the whole treasure as a present. The gold was valued at about three

[1] *C. I. L.* VI. 1703.

thousand dollars. Flaminio Galgano, a contemporary of Matteo da Castello, was equally fortunate. While quarrying stone at the foot of the hill near S. Prisca, he discovered in the heart of the rock a square room, with the pavement inlaid with pieces of agate and cornelian, and the walls covered with panels of gilt copper, in the cornice of which rare medals were set as a motive of decoration. The room contained many paterae and instruments of sacrifice, all damaged by fire.

Pietro Sante Bartoli, in his Memoirs (n. 128), gives the following account of another find, probably associated with the same barbarian invasion : " When Urban VIII. built the Bastione del Priorato di Malta, in front of the church of S. Maria Aventina, many curious things were discovered. Among them was a hiding-place, formed by two walls, inside of which was concealed a silver table service, worked in *repoussé*. The place of concealment was covered and screened from view by a piece of a marble cornice, since removed to the Villa Pamfili. Another treasure of gold coins, rings, and other precious objects was found inside an earthen jar; the police, acting under the orders of Cardinal Antonio Barberini, sought far and wide for the finder, but they could never lay hands on him. A few days after, another workman from Aquila discovered a leaden box, and, although his pay for several weeks of labour was still to his credit, he thought it better to abscond with the box than to wait for his money."

Perhaps the most remarkable set of silverware ever buried in Rome for fear of barbarian plundering is the one discovered between June, 1793, and March of the following year, under the convent of the Paolotte, on the Via di S. Lucia in Selce, the ancient Clivus Suburanus. The collection, which belonged to the toilet-service of a lady of rank, weighed 1029 ounces, and comprised a *pyxis* inscribed with the names of Turcius Asterius Secundus and of his wife Projecta, two candlesticks in the shape of brackets, five plates and four soup-plates, with the name "Projecta Turci," in gold-niello, five goblets in the shape of ewers, a wash-basin in the shape of a shell, and lamps, forks, and spoons, together with remains of a sedan chair and sundry other articles, the catalogue of which is given by Ennio Quirino Visconti.[1] Pius VI. allowed the treasure to be disposed of by sale. A few pieces were bought by Carlo Gherardi, and resold to Baron von Kevenhuller; all the rest were purchased by Baron von Schellersheim. The finest objects are now exhibited in the British Museum, thanks to the generosity of the late Sir Augustus Franks. The silver set was evidently hidden in great haste. Visconti affirms that he saw a piece of a linen towel inside the shell-shaped basin, "a proof," he says, "of the hurry with which the treasure was buried." The concealment must have

[1] *Lettera di Ennio Quirino Visconti intorno ad una antica supellettile d'argento*, etc. 2d ed. Rome, 1827, xxv. plates.

taken place after 362 A.D., when Turcius Asterius Secundus was prefect of the City, and in fact after his death, because some of the pieces bear the name of a Peregrina, who seems to have been his daughter. We are not far, therefore, from the date of the sack of 410. The question naturally suggests itself: Why this collection of valuables, and many others concealed at the same time and for the same cause, were not dug out and recovered after the retreat of the barbarians? The inquiry is more easily raised than answered. Perhaps the one or two persons who knew the secret lost their lives in the sack of 410; possibly the palace of the Asterii was burnt to the ground, and all access to the hiding-place cut off.

The barbarian invasions had one result which, from the archaeological point of view, is of even greater significance than the burying of treasure: I refer to the careful hiding of bronze statues in times of panic in order to save them from injury or destruction, thus making possible their rediscovery in modern times in a perfect state of preservation. Of course, in many instances, we are not able to determine whether the concealment took place in 410 rather than in 455 or 537, or some other year. What we do know is, that bronzes were hidden through fear of an imminent calamity; and the presumption is in favour of the earlier date because the number of bronze statues in existence must have been vastly diminished after the first sacking of the City.

It has been suggested that fear of the Christians, on account of the acts of violence occasionally committed by the populace against the temples and their contents, may have been the cause that led to the concealment of images, particularly of the gods; but deeds of violence against pagan sanctuaries — not uncommon in the East, as in the case of the destruction of the magnificent Serapeum at Alexandria in 391 — were extremely rare in Rome. The rough painting in one of the catacombs of the Via Salaria Vetus which represents the overthrowing of a statue[1] is unique in its way; and though St. Augustine[2] speaks of "the overthrowing of all the images in the City of Rome," his words, obviously metaphorical, are contradicted by Claudianus,[3] who, writing in the year 403, mentions vast multitudes of bronze and marble statues, lining the streets and the forums.[4]

Statues were sometimes concealed by the magistrates themselves. Two inscriptions, one of which was discovered at Benevento, the other at Capua, describe the reërection of works of statuary, *reperta in abditis locis*, or *translata ex abditis locis*. I have described elsewhere[5]

[1] De Rossi, *Bull. di arch. crist.*, 1865, pp. 3, 4.

[2] Augustine, *Sermo cv de verbis evang. Luc.* X. 13.

[3] *De vi. consulatu Honorii*, 42.

[4] Fuller information on this subject will be found in Edmund Le Blant's paper, "De quelques statues cachées par les anciens," published in *Compte-rendus de l'Acad. des Inscriptions*, 1890, p. 541; and in Grisar's *I papi del Medio Evo*, ital. edit. of 1897, Vol. I. p. 38.

[5] *Ruins and Excavations*, p. 456.

the discovery of the bronze Hercules Invictus which had been hidden by the charioteers of the Circus Maximus, and of the Hercules Magnus Custos concealed by those of the Circus Flaminius; the first came to light in the time of Sixtus IV. (1471-1484), the second in 1864. This last had been carefully buried in a kind of coffin made of slabs of portasanta. The bronze gladiator, likewise, discovered in March, 1885, in the foundations of the Teatro Drammatico on the Via Nazionale, had not been buried in haste in that heap of rubbish, but had been treated with the utmost care. The figure, which was in a sitting posture, had been poised on a stone capital, as upon a stool, and the trench, which had been dug under the platform of the temple of the Sun to conceal the statue, had been filled with finely sifted earth, in order to save the bronze from any possible injury.

As a rule, the bronzes discovered in Rome since the Renaissance — I speak of this later period because our knowledge of earlier finds is too imperfect and fragmentary to be of value — had been carefully hidden, or even thrown into the Tiber, in times of panic. The secret of the place of hiding was lost, either on account of the death of those who knew the spot, or because the great masses of débris had made it impossible to reach it again.

Many of these places of concealment have been found in our days; three of them deserve special mention.

FIG. 14. — Bronze heads found in 1880 under the English church, Via del Babuino.

1. Augustus.   2. Nero.
3, 4. Portrait head of the first century — name unknown.

The first is the treasure-trove unearthed in 1849, a few weeks before the storming of Rome by the French army under General Oudinot, beneath the house at No. 17, Vicolo delle Palme, now Vicolo dell' Atleta. It consisted of a marble copy of the bronze Apoxyomenos of Lysippus; of the bronze horse, now in the Palazzo dei Conservatori, described by Emil Braun as "an unique work, a masterpiece, and a genuine Grecian antique"; of a bronze foot with a particularly ornamental caliga, which may possibly have belonged to the rider of the horse; of a bronze bull, and many other fragments of less importance.

The second discovery was made September 15, 1880, at the corner of the Via del Babuino and Via del Gesù e Maria where the English Church of All Saints was in process of erection.[1] The bronzes lay nineteen feet below the threshold of the main door. There was a head of more than life size, which was thought to represent Augustus, and to have some connexion with the mausoleum of that Emperor; a head of Nero with the eyes perforated, and several busts of unknown personages of the first century.

The third discovery took place about the same time at the corner of the Via Nazionale and Via di S. Eufemia, while the Marchesa Capranica del Grillo (Madame Ristori) was laying the foundations of her city house. The treasure consisted of marbles and

[1] *Bull. Com.*, 1881, p. 30, pl. i.

bronzes. The latter rank among the best specimens of Greco-Roman art, if indeed they are not purely Greek. There was a sitting statue of Cybele, holding a diminutive millstone in the left hand; the mouth of a fountain in the shape of a lion's head, and the head of a youth, the most superb piece of bronze work I have ever seen. These bronzes all soon disappeared, and I have never been able to find out what became of them.

Another consequence of the Gothic invasion was the abandonment of the Catacombs. Christian archaeologists have stated that burials in the Catacombs, very rare between 400 and 410 on account of the insecurity of the suburbs, were given up altogether after 410. The reason for this abandonment is easily seen. The storming of Alaric marks, thus, the end of a great and glorious era in the history of "underground Rome"; it put an end altogether to the work of the *fossores*.

After suffering more damage in the invasion of 457, the Catacombs were irreparably devastated in 537, during the siege of the Goths under Vitiges. It is distinctly stated by the biographer of Pope Silverius (536–537) that "churches and tombs of martyrs were destroyed by the Goths"; but it is not easy for us to understand why the Goths, bigoted Christians as they were and full of respect for the basilicas of St. Peter and St. Paul, as Procopius declares, should have ransacked the Catacombs and have violated the tombs of martyrs, breaking up their commemorative inscriptions.

Perhaps they could not read Latin or Greek epitaphs, and so were unable to make a distinction between pagan and Christian cemeteries; perhaps they were hunting for hidden treasures, or the relics of saints.

Whatever may have been the reason of their behaviour, it is certainly a significant fact that at least two encampments of the Goths in 537 were just over the Catacombs and around their entrances; one on the Via Salaria, over the Catacombs of Thrason, and the other on the Via Labicana, over those of Peter and Marcellinus. The barbarians, naturally, could hardly resist the temptation to explore those subterranean wonders; indeed, they were obliged to do so by the most elementary rules of precaution. In each of the two catacombs mentioned, a memorial tablet has been found commemorating the repairs made in haste by Pope Vigilius between March, 537, the date of the retreat of Vitiges, and the following November, the date of the journey of Vigilius to Constantinople.[1] Traces of this Pope's restorations have been found also in other catacombs, especially in those of Callixtus and Hippolytus. His example was followed by private individuals. The tomb of Crysanthus and Daria, in the Via Salaria, was repaired after the retreat of the barbarians *pauperis ex censu*, with the modest means of one of the humbler followers of the Master.

Notwithstanding the feeling of insecurity caused by

[1] Cf. *Pagan and Christian Rome*, p. 324.

the sack of 410, the body of the Emperor Honorius, who died at Ravenna, August 15, 423, was not interred in that city, but was transported to Rome and given burial in the imperial mausoleum which had been raised on the south side of St. Peter's Church, in wretched imitation of the great structures of Augustus and Hadrian. This tomb of the decadence was composed of two round halls, joined by a covered passage. Each rotunda contained six or seven recesses, in which the imperial sarcophagi were placed. Mention of the structure with its genuine denomination of *mosileos* (mausoleum) occurs in the life of Stephen II. (752 A.D.), who placed in the western chambers the remains of Petronilla, the supposed daughter of St. Peter, whence it derived its mediaeval name of S. Petronilla; the other rotunda was known as the chapel of St. Andrew, and also of "Our Lady of the Fever." The first building was destroyed in the first quarter of the sixteenth century, to make room for the south transept of the new basilica, where the chapel of Saints Simon and Judas now stands; the other met with a similar fate during the pontificate of Pius VI., and its place was occupied by the new sacristy. The architecture of the *mosileos*, so similar to that of the tomb of St. Helena (the Torre Pignattara) on the Via Labicana, gives us the measure of the decline of Roman art and civilisation, when we compare it with the imposing mausoleums of Augustus and Hadrian.

The robbery of the imperial graves which filled the two rotundas by St. Peter's was accomplished at various times and by various persons. It excels, in refinement of barbarous and useless destruction, all the other deeds of the unscrupulous age in which it occurred. The first desecration dates from 1458; the second took place in 1519; the last, in 1544. The unique set of crown jewels of the fifth century was sent to the mint, or sold or given away. With the exception of a *bulla* inscribed with the names of Honorius and his empress Maria, daughter of Stilicho and Serena, and sister of Thermantia and Eucherius, which is now in the hands of Prince Trivulzio of Milan, every other specimen has disappeared or lost its identity.

CHAPTER VI

THE SACK OF ROME BY THE VANDALS IN 455

THE exact date of the second capture of Rome, by Genseric and the Vandals, is not known, but it was probably the beginning of June, 455, three days after the murder of Petronius Maximus, who had himself caused the death of Valentinian III., and usurped the throne. The Vandals, with whom were mixed Bedouins and Moors, entered the City by the Porta Portuensis, and plundered it at leisure for the space of fourteen days. The booty was carted off methodically to the ships moored alongside the quays, now called La Marmorata and Ripa grande. The palace of the Caesars, which Valentinian III., unlike his predecessors, had constantly occupied and had kept in repair, was stripped even of its commonest furniture. The temple of Jupiter Optimus Maximus, who from the lofty summit of the Capitoline hill had presided over the destinies of the Roman Commonwealth since the time of the Tarquins, was also put to ransom; its statues and votive offerings were carried off to adorn the African residence of Genseric, and half the roof was stripped of its tiles of gilt bronze. It is also reported that the trophies of the Jewish war, represented in the bas-reliefs of the arch of Titus and deposited by him in the temple of Peace, fell into the hands of the barbarians. These spoils, as well as the massive gold plate plundered from the Roman churches, were discovered at Carthage, eighty years later, by Belisarius, and carried back in triumph, not to Rome, but to Constantinople.

We have a memorial of these eventful days in the Basilica Eudoxiana, now the church of S. Pietro in Vincoli, which was built by Eudoxia the younger, widow of Valentinian III., and a victim, first, of the usurper Maximus, and then of Genseric. This beautiful church is built with columns of Greek marble taken from one of the neighbouring edifices, perhaps the Baths of Titus or of Trajan, or the Porticus Tellurensis — a fact which shows how little respect was paid by the members of the imperial families to the laws concerning the preservation of ancient buildings. The edict of Maiorianus, issued at Ravenna in 458, forbidding once more the dismantling of ancient structures for the erection of new ones, confirms our belief that the former had come to be looked upon as stone quarries.

I cannot undertake here to speak with more detail of the consequences of the sack of the Vandals, as regards the fate of buildings and works of art, for the reason that exact information is wanting. In most cases we are not in a position to know whether certain results followed this invasion, or those of later date. Nor does it fall within my province to recount the history of the City for the half-century after the storming of Genseric, — truly a harrowing narrative of siege, famine, pillage, massacre, fires, and pestilence. In general we may assume that the last half of the fifth century was almost as disastrous a period for the history of the Roman monuments as it was for the wretched inhabitants.

CHAPTER VII

THE CITY IN THE SIXTH CENTURY

AT the opening of the sixth century the prevailing gloom is penetrated, and thrown into even stronger contrast, by a ray of light. A new era seemed to dawn with the accession of Theoderic, whose enlightened administration (500–526) gave itself no little concern for the remains of Rome's greatness. On the day of his arrival in Rome Theoderic addressed kind words to the people from the rostra in front of the Senate-house (*in loco qui Palma aurea dicitur*), and then proceeded to the palace of the Caesars. The provisions made by this Prince for the improvement of the City are recorded in the *Variae* of his secretary, Cassiodorius. He appointed a body of engineers and architects to superintend the restoration of public edifices, under the direction of an *architectus publicorum*, and as we have already seen he revived the office of the "keeper of statues." The theatre of Pompey was repaired with the help of one of the great men of the age, Avianius Symmachus; the Coliseum, with the help of Decius Marius Venantius Basilius, prefect of the City in the year 508. The duty of putting the aqueducts in order, and keeping the baths and the fountains well supplied with water was entrusted to a *comes formarum urbis;* the care of public sewers to a sanitary engineer named Johannes; the charge of the harbour of Rome was given to a harbour-master (*comes portus urbis Romae*), assisted by a deputy (*vicarius*); the theatres and other buildings designed for public shows were placed under the superintendence of a "supervisor of amusements" (*tribunus voluptatum*). Thus thoroughgoing repairs were made, not at the expense of other edifices, as in the case of the predecessors of Theoderic, but with brick expressly prepared in the great old brickyard called Portus Licini. They were all stamped — in this case appropriately, we must acknowledge — with the inscription —

REGNANTE D · N · THEODERICO FELIX ROMA

I have never made or witnessed an excavation on the site of any of the great buildings of Rome without discovering one or more of Theoderic's bricks. The style of masonry which prevailed in his time can best be examined in the repairs made to the "arcus Caelimontani," the branch aqueduct supplying the imperial palace in the Via di S. Stefano Rotondo. The sums destined for such works were derived from local taxation. Maximian of Ravenna states in his annals that the two hundred pounds of gold set aside for the restoration of the walls of the City and of the imperial residence were collected from the city tax on wine — which at this day remains one of the chief sources of revenue for the municipal treasury. The churches of St. Pancras on the Via Aurelia and of S. Martino ai Monti date from the time of this benevolent ruler.

In describing the siege of Vitiges, which lasted from February, 537, to March, 538, and the intrenched camps raised by the Goths around the beleaguered City, Procopius refers to the cutting of the aqueducts in the following words (*De Bello Goth.* I. 19): "The Goths having thus surrounded the City, broke down the aqueducts to cut off the supply of water. Rome has fourteen aqueducts . . . and their channels are so high and broad that a horseman could easily ride through them." This statement is erroneous in two respects: the aqueducts were in reality not fourteen but eleven, — Appia, Anio Vetus, Marcia, Tepula, Julia, Virgo, Alsietina, Claudia, Anio Novus, Trajana, Alexandrina; and their channels "could not be entered even by a pygmy riding on a goat or a ram."[1]

Belisarius walled up the mouths of the aqueducts, in order to prevent the enemy from making them a means of entering the City. The consequences of the cutting were not so serious as to cause a water famine, because there were enough springs within the walls to meet the emergency of the moment, not to speak of

[1] Fabretti, *De aquis*, p. 145: *ne Pygmaei quidem, arietis, capraeve dorso insidentis, quales eos describit Plinius, capaces fuerunt.*

the Tiber, the water of which has always been considered potable and wholesome. It is also necessary to observe that, after the removal of the imperial Court to Constantinople, the water supply of Rome had lost much of its world-famous purity and wholesomeness. Any one can convince himself of the truth of this statement by examining the channel of the Marcia, the purest and best of Roman waters, at the Ponte degli Arci at the foot of Monte Arcese, near Tivoli, or that of the Claudia, which in purity ranked next to the Marcia,[1] near the Colle Monitola between Tivoli and Castel Madama. The following section of the channel, which I made at Monte Arcese, May 5, 1881, will indicate the real state of the case better than any description (Fig. 15).

The channel (*specus*) measured originally six and one-half feet (2.05 metres) in height, that is, to the base of the vaulted ceiling, and three and one-third feet (1.01 metres) in breadth. As long as the aqueduct was well taken care of by the *curatores aquarum* and their staff of subordinate officers, the dimensions of the channel and its capacity did not perceptibly diminish. There are, on the sides and the bottom, thin layers of alabastrine purity and transparency, which may have been formed in the golden age of Roman administration; but they hardly exceed half an inch in thickness. The deposits, however, formed at the time of the bar-

[1] Frontinus, I. 13: *quae bonitatis proximae est Marciae.*

barian invasions and in consequence of the abandonment of the aqueducts, are fourteen inches thick, the free channel being thus reduced from six and a half to a little more than four feet (1.65 metres) in height, and to a width of less than a foot. These deposits are of every colour and quality, containing carbonate of lime of spongy texture, mud, clay, and a conglomerate of gravel. Another curious instance of the neglect of the aqueducts after the middle of the fourth century is to be seen in the Vigna di S. Croce in Gerusalemme, as you enter by the first gate on the left of that church. The water dripping through the joints of the stones, of which the channel is built, was so saturated with

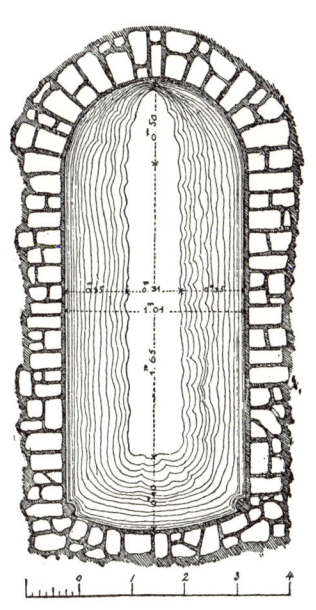

FIG. 15.—Section of the channel of the Aqua Marcia, at Monte Arcese, showing deposits on the bottom and sides.

deposits of lime that the whole height of the arcades was covered with incrustations, and came to have the appearance of a great rock honeycombed with cavities.

Although the inhabitants of Rome were not immediately affected by a water famine, in other respects the cutting off of the water supply by the barbarians proved disastrous to the City as well as to the country around it. In the City it led to the abandonment of the great imperial thermae, which King Theoderic had just tried to put into repair. The same fate was shared by the artificial basins called *stagna* or *euripi*, and by the 1212 public fountains and 247 reservoirs which had adorned and supplied the City in earlier days. The higher quarters suffered the most, because their water supply, borne many miles on stone or brick arcades, could be more easily stopped. The supply of the lower quarters, on the other hand, was never diverted for any great length of time, because the channels of the Virgo, of the Appia, and of the Anio Vetus, which fed the Campus Martius, ran mostly underground and could be repaired without difficulty. This is the reason why the more salubrious hills were abandoned toward the end of the fifth century, not to be inhabited again until the time of Sixtus V., who in 1587 made life upon them possible again with the building of his Acquedotto Felice.

One incident of the Gothic siege of 537, connected with the fate of the aqueducts, is described by Procopius as follows: " Between the Latin and the Appian Ways there still exist two aqueducts (the Claudian and the Marcian), supported by massive arches. At the fiftieth furlong from Rome (at the place now called the Torre Fiscale), they join and cross each other in such a way that the one which was on the right now diverges to the left. After a short distance they meet and cross again, and each follows its original course. The space between the two crossings is therefore entirely surrounded by aqueducts, the lower arches of which were filled up by the barbarians with stones and mud, so as to form a regular fortification, within which they remained encamped, to the number of at least seven thousand, in order to prevent any kind of provisions from entering the City. . . . With this as a base of operations, the Goths occupied themselves with despoiling and ravaging the Campagna. . . . They remained there a long time, and were only driven out by the plague."[1]

De Rossi has collected important proofs of the accuracy of this portion of the narrative of Procopius. Describing the sepulchral crypt, found by Fortunati in 1876, at the fifth mile-stone of the Via Latina, on Prince Torlonia's farm (Roma Vecchia), he says: "In this very quarter of the suburbs I located the *campus barbaricus*, where the Goths intrenched themselves in the sixth century, and I suspected that the bodies, which bore traces of having perished by a violent death, and which were lying very near the surface quite close to the Torlonia tomb, were those of this warlike horde. In the Torlonia tomb itself we found, on the skull of one of the skeletons, evident traces of an oblique cut, inflicted by a sword or some similar weapon."

"In 1853," De Rossi continues, "by the side of the

[1] *De Bello Goth.* II. 3.

modern road to Albano, between the fourth and the fifth mile-stone, I was present at the discovery of tombs, made with simple marble slabs, and of a sarcophagus. . . . The corpses had been enveloped in rich cloth, of which, at the first moment of uncovering, we saw traces in the form of gold and purple threads. . . . Then not far off, just beneath the surface, we saw a series of coffins made of stones and tiles collected at random, filled with skeletons of men, the loins and breasts bound with broad bands, which looked as if they had been saturated with blood, and these we thought to have been soldiers killed in action. . . . This discovery recalled to my mind an episode in the Gothic war (as described by Procopius) which made fearful havoc among the neighbouring villas. In the records of Gregory II. mention is made of a '*Massa Camustis iuxta campum barbaricum ex corpore patrimonii Appiae.*'"

It is easy to picture to ourselves what damage was done to this once fertile and smiling part of the Campagna, and to the aqueducts that traversed it, especially to the Claudia, the most conspicuous of them all. Yet it is but just to observe that the barbarians damaged the aqueducts only so far as was necessary to stop the flow of the water; we have no reason to suppose that they threw down great arches and pilasters simply for the pleasure of destruction — that would have been mere lost labour. These wonderful creations of Roman hydraulic skill, these triumphal arcades crossing the Campagna in every direction and distributing everywhere fertility and health, were destroyed, as were so many other monuments, by the Romans themselves, in times much nearer to our own than is ordinarily supposed.

We have reason to believe that in 1585, when the construction of the Acquedotto Felice was decreed by Sixtus V., the series of arcades of the Marcia and of the Claudia (Fig. 20), both seven miles long, were practically intact. Matteo da Castello, first, and, after his resignation, Domenico Fontana, laid hands on the noble structures, burning their travertine blocks into lime, splitting and hammering those of tufa and peperino for use in the new aqueduct. Whatever remains were left standing became the prey of local land-owners, especially of the trustees of the hospital of S. Giovanni, in whose archives I have found documents concerning the sale at public auction of the stone arch, over which the Claudia spanned the Via Latina near the farmhouse of Roma Vecchia; and again, the sale of four piers of peperino to Bartolomeo Vitali, of two to the brothers Guidotti, and so on.[1] Three or four hundred feet of the channel of the same aqueduct were destroyed by the owner of the farm of the Capannelle in 1887; the Mediterranean Railway Company, which, about the same time, built the new line to Segni, is responsible for other damages.

[1] Lanciani, *I Comentarii di Frontino*, p. 149.

A walk from the Porta Furba (on the road to Frascati) to the Porta Maggiore, by the Vicolo del Mandrione, will give the student a melancholy appreciation of the importance and of the fate of the Roman aqueducts,

FIG. 16. — The remains of the Claudian aqueduct at the Porta Furba.

which, after so many centuries of spoliation, are still among the most impressive remains of ancient Rome (Fig. 16).

Notwithstanding the ravages of the Vandals and the desperate straits of the people of Rome on many occasions since the first sack of the Goths, Procopius, whom I have already quoted so often, speaks of a number of monuments as standing uninjured toward the middle of the sixth century. We learn from him that the City in general, and the Forum especially, retained an imposing array of bronze and marble statues, the works of Phidias and Lysippus; that the celebrated Cow of Myron was yet to be seen above the fountain in the Forum of Peace; that the bronze statue of Janus, five cubits high, was still preserved in the cella of his four-faced temple; and that the group of the Three Fates — the one, probably, which Pliny classifies among the earliest works of the kind in Rome — still gave the name of *Tria Fata* to the north corner of the Forum by the Senate-house.

The same historian describes how one of the Gothic camps had been established in the Gaianum, a circus or hippodrome of the gardens of Domitia, and how the Greek garrison of the mole of Hadrian hurled upon its assailants many statues which even to that time had ornamented this fortified mausoleum. " Of all the people in the world," he concludes (IV. 22), " the Romans love their City and its historical monuments the best. Although fallen a prey to barbarian invaders so many times, they have succeeded in keeping up many of their great buildings, and preserving relics connected with the origin and foundation of their City. Among these last I can mention a large canoe hollowed out of the trunk of a tree, which they preserve in the arsenal on the left bank of the Tiber, as the one used by Aeneas in reaching the Latin shore."

In the year 590, which was that of the election of Pope Gregory the Great (September 3), Rome seems to have reached the extremity of misfortune. An inundation of the Tiber, at the end of the previous year, had caused the ruin of some temples and monuments and of innumerable private dwellings, and the flood was, as usual, followed by famine and pestilence. The beautiful legend of the angel seen above the mausoleum of Hadrian in the act of sheathing his sword, while Gregory at the head of the panic-stricken population was proceeding in pilgrimage to St. Peter's (a memorial of the vision still remains in the bronze figure on the top of the Castel S. Angelo), marks really the first change for the better in the fortunes of Rome. By Rome I mean the City itself protected by the walls of Aurelian and Honorius; for the surrounding district was incessantly devastated by the Lombards of Agilulf and Ariulf, and its inhabitants murdered or driven away.

CHAPTER VIII

BURIAL PLACES WITHIN AND WITHOUT THE WALLS

FROM a remote period, burial within the city limits was prohibited by Roman law. Yet many graves have been found within the walls, and Nibby has suggested that the first infringement of the early enactment, the first interments *intra muros*, must be regarded as a consequence of the siege of Vitiges.

Earlier instances of the practice, however, are not lacking. Tombs dating from the time of Theoderic (493-526 A.D.) have been found in the Praetorian camp, in the gardens of Sallust, and in the graveyard of S. Giacomo del Colosseo. Those of the Praetorian camp were seen by Lupi, in the first quarter of the last century, within the cells which line the north side of the quadrangle; those of the gardens of Sallust were seen by De Rossi, in 1869, in that part of the Vigna Barberini-Spithoever which is now crossed by the Via Flavia and the Via Aureliana.

The exploration of the graveyard by the Coliseum began in the spring of 1895, and its results are described at length in the *Bullettino Comunale* of the same year. There were two or three layers of tombs, — the oldest, at the same level with the amphitheatre, dating from the time of Theoderic, the latest dating from the beginning of the seventh century. One of the later tombs, discovered opposite the thirty-third arcade, is now exhibited in the Museo Municipale on the Caelian Hill. The inscription gives the names of a Fortunatus and Lucia and of their little daughter Gemmula, and ends with the warning, "Whoever shall violate or injure this tomb, may he share the fate of Judas!" No wonder: the grave stood right in the middle of a thoroughfare, which, even in those days, must have been crowded.

The two precious basins, one of green and one of reddish basalt, removed toward the end of the last century from the Baths of Caracalla to the Cortile di Belvedere of the Vatican Museum, had both been used for coffins. A sepulchral vault containing many hundred bodies was discovered in the Baths of Constantine;[1] another, in the remains of other baths in the Vigna Grimani (Barberini).[2] In the course of time each of the Roman churches — and there were several hundred of them — came to possess a local graveyard. We cannot excavate anywhere in Rome without coming across one of them. I have seen, and in several instances have myself explored, cemeteries belonging to the church of S. Maria ad Martyres (the Pantheon); of S. Marcello, of S. Nicola in Calcarario,

[1] Vacca, *Mem.* 112.   [2] Bartoli, *Mem.* 31.

of S. Maria in Campitelli, of S. Sebastiano in Pallara, of S. Ciriaco de Camilliano, of S. Maria Nuova, and others. The largest of all, attached to the hospital of S. Maria delle Grazie, occupied one half of the Basilica Julia, the layer of human remains being from six to eight feet in thickness.

The Catacombs, as we have seen, were abandoned in 410; but what was the fate of the pagan tombs and mausoleums which lined the highroads in every direction beyond the limits of the City? I wish that I could summarise here the information given on this subject by that indefatigable explorer of Roman tombs, Francesco Ficoroni, in his work, *La Bolla d'oro dei fanciulli romani*, Part II. ;[1] as it is I can only mention a few points.

The family vaults, Ficoroni remarks, were generally composed of a room or enclosed place on a level with the road, where the funeral banquets and the anniversary gatherings took place, and of a crypt where the ashes were kept in urns, or the bodies laid to rest in richly carved marble sarcophagi. The former, standing above ground, and within easy reach of the passer-by, must have been stripped of their valuable contents at a very early period, perhaps even before the first inroad of Alaric. When there was nothing else of value left, the Romans attacked the very walls of which the tombs were built, the porticoes, colonnades, and roofs,

[1] *Diversità dei mausolei romani, loro diroccamento*, etc.

for the sake of the marble, which they wanted for their lime-kilns. This process of burning the marbles of sepulchral monuments for lime became so common that the emperors had to enact capital punishment as a penalty against the offenders. In 349, sixty-one years before Alaric's invasion, the Emperor Constans substituted a heavy fine for capital punishment.[1]

These imperial provisions may have saved from destruction for a few years longer the mausoleums more exposed to view; but those standing back from the highroads, screened by trees or by the undulations of the ground, probably disappeared faster than ever. I speak, of course, of the general rule, because among the three or four hundred thousand tombs which encircled the City, there were, to be sure, some remarkable exceptions. A few of them, conspicuous for their size and for their wealth in marble and travertine, have survived to the present day, as the mausoleums of Caecilia Metella and of Lucilius Paetus, and the tombs of Vibius Marianus (Fig. 17) and of Vergilius Eurysaces.

The underground rooms, or hypogaea, suffered less damage. Search was made, either by the degenerate Romans or by the barbarians, for the valuable objects buried with the corpse, or placed as a memento in the cinerary urns, such as ear-rings, finger-rings, and brooches (*fibulae*); but the urns themselves, the beauti-

[1] See his constitution to Limenius in the *Codex Theodosianus*, X. Tit. 17, *de sepulchris violatis*.

ful sarcophagi, the glass and terra cotta vessels peculiar to columbaria, and even the bronze lamps and candelabras, were often left undisturbed. This is the reason why the excavation of our ancient cemeteries is rich in finds, as I can testify from personal observation.

FIG. 17. — Tomb of P. Vibius Marianus, so-called "Tomb of Nero," on the Via Clodia, 4½ miles north of Rome.

My first experience in the exploration of tombs dates from 1868, when those lining the Via Severiana, between Ostia and Castel Fusano, were first opened by the elder Visconti (Fig. 18). They yielded a great quantity of glassware and exquisite Arezzo cups, besides a few objects in gold and enamel. Next in date and importance came the exploration of the columbaria of the

Statilian family, in that portion of the Esquiline cemetery which extends from the so-called Minerva Medica to the Porta Maggiore (1875). In the space of a few weeks, and within an area of a few thousand square feet, we recovered 566 inscriptions, and many hundred

FIG. 18. — Columbarium on the Via Severiana, near Ostia, opened in 1868.

objects in terra cotta, glass, bone, ivory, bronze, gold, silver, and precious marbles.

Ficoroni has offered an ingenious suggestion in regard to the engraved gems or cameos which are found loose in the earth in great numbers within a circuit of three or four miles from the walls. After stating that out of ninety-two sepulchral chambers, which he had excavated in the Vigna Moroni by the Porta S. Sebastiano, between 1705 and 1709, only one had not been searched before, he says: "I found in the unopened urns, among the charred bones, a few necklaces, ear-rings, and finger-rings, and a piece of jewelry with sapphires. My workmen, however, in sifting the earth which filled up or covered these columbaria, and also the open passages between them, found a great many cameos and intaglios in precious stones, broken or indented around the edge. These stones are constantly found in the vineyards and orchards which extend over the old cemeteries; and as they still show traces of the hard glue, by means of which they were fastened to their sockets, it seems to me that they must have been taken out and thrown away as a useless encumbrance by those who were seeking for gold alone. What possible value could engraved stones represent in the eyes of the Romans of the fifth century, or of their invaders?"

This general rifling of burial crypts is the more surprising if we recall the precautions taken in many cases to conceal the entrances to them. After the last occupant had been laid to rest, and the sarcophagi or urns sealed with brass clamps and molten lead, the door was walled up with stones or blocks of marble, resembling in colour and shape those with which the rest of the mausoleum was covered; and every trace of an entrance was then made to disappear. This is the reason why some crypts, rich in funereal decoration, have escaped molestation until a comparatively recent period. The secret passage leading to the tomb of Caecilia Metella was discovered by accident, in the time of Paul III. (1534–1550), by a stone-cutter engaged in wrenching away the blocks of travertine from the square foundation. The beautiful sarcophagus found in the inner chamber is still to be seen in the palace of that Pope. A similar discovery, under Alexander VII. (1655–1667), took place also in connexion with the pyramid of C. Cestius, the entrance to which was so artfully disguised that it could be located only by the hollow sound of the stones with which it had been blocked. The grave-robbers, however, have avoided the difficulty, in nine cases out of ten, by boring a hole through the core of the monument toward its centre.

Most of the sepulchral chambers discovered in my time had been plundered in this way. The best instance can be seen in the beautiful crypt at the second mile-stone of the Via Latina, called "Sepolcro degli stucchi," from the well-preserved bas-reliefs in plaster, representing nymphs and nereids driving sea-monsters, which ornament its vaulted ceiling. The door leading into this chamber was found to be undisturbed; but a hole could be seen in the ceiling, hardly two feet in diameter, by means of which the plunderers had effected their descent, and carried away the spoils (Fig. 19). The marble sarcophagi had been carefully searched, some by the removal of the lids, found lying in pieces on the floor, some by means of a hole made in the side of the coffin.

Fig. 19. — The Sepolcro degli Stucchi, showing the hole made by plunderers in the vaulted ceiling.

I may close this chapter by reminding the reader that from the time of Boniface VIII., who instituted the Giubileo in 1300, to the end of the last century, the highroads followed by the pilgrims on the way to Rome were repaired every twenty-fifth year, at the expense of the tombs lining the road on either side. The information which I have collected on this point will be published in Vols. III. and IV. of my *Storia degli Scavi di Roma.*

FIG. 20.—View of the Campagna. In the distance, remains of the Claudian Aqueduct, cut by Vitiges, and exploited in modern times for building materials.

CHAPTER IX

THE DEVASTATION AND DESERTION OF THE CAMPAGNA

THE final desolation of the Campagna, with its concomitant, the plague of malaria, dates from the time of Gregory the Great (590–604). Villas and farmhouses were set fire to, olive orchards and vineyards uprooted, the supply of water cut off; all sources of life and thrift were drained, and the whole plain from the Apennines to the sea was turned into an unhealthful and dangerous wilderness.

Whenever a Roman villa has been excavated in these last years, I have paid special attention to the stratification of its ruins, as the only means of finding out what the cause of its destruction was. There are, as a general rule, three strata. The uppermost consists of vegetable soil, produced by the disintegration of the ruins themselves, by the decomposition of the trees, bushes, and grass, and by earth deposited by atmospheric agencies. The middle stratum is made up of building materials, such as brick, blocks of tufa, tufa prisms for reticulate work, plaster, cement, and fragments of marble veneering. The lowest, lying directly over the marble or mosaic floor, is composed almost exclusively of roof tiles and roofing materials. From this relation of parts we infer that, whether the villas perished by fire, or by natural decay and abandonment, the first part to fall in was the roof, the remains of which, for that reason, lie upon the pavements. The walls must have fallen decades, if not centuries, later, because there is always a thin layer of vegetable soil between the remains of the roof and those of the walls.

The walls have generally fallen toward the same point of the compass, as if thrown down by an earthquake; and a similar observation has been made in regard to the columns of the peristyles. One thing is certain: that when the roofs fell, whether by natural decay or by the violence of man, the marble statues which adorned the villa, its terraces, its nymphaea, and its colonnades were still *in situ*, and in some cases were still standing on their pedestals. The herms at the crossings of the garden avenues, the exquisite carved fountains, the portrait-busts of the atria, remained likewise uninjured, and so they would have remained to the present day had it not been for the lime-burners of the early Renaissance, and for the contractors for the maintenance of the highroads, who in this respect have caused incalculable damage; more works of art have been destroyed in the last five centuries than in all the centuries of barbarian plundering.

For the same reason, the few villas which, on account

of their secluded location and safe distance from the highroads, escaped the mediaeval and Renaissance plunderers, prove to be a perfect mine of statuary. I have collected some remarkable documents on this point which will be published later. Let me quote two instances, one from the Villa Quintiliorum on the Appian Way, the other from the Villa Voconiorum near Marino, the ancient Castrimoenium.

The Villa Quintiliorum, the picturesque remains of which are now called S. Maria Nova, from the church and monastery of that name, which owned them in past ages, has been excavated at least eight times, with such good results that a section of the farm is actually called *Statuario*, " mine of statuary." The oldest search dates from the pontificate of Innocent VIII., more precisely, from April 16, 1485. It led to the discovery of the body of the so-called Tulliola, still retaining the rosy colour of the flesh and lifelike appearance.[1] Several inscriptions, sarcophagi, and sepulchral monuments came to light on the same occasion. The tomb of the Apusii was found in the following century. Winckelmann, who was present at the excavations of 1762 made by Cardinal Alessandro Albani, describes the finding of a beautiful marble basin, thirty-five palms in circumference, with the Labours of Hercules in alto-relievo; of a portico, of the areostyle type, with columns of the Ionic order, and of a wall covered with frescoes.

[1] See *Pagan and Christian Rome,* p. 295.

Here also, in 1780, Giovanni Volpato discovered several columns of bigio and breccia corallina, thirteen feet high; the colossal head of Julia Domna, the Ganymede, and the "Antiochia," now in the Vatican Museum; besides the statue of a young Caesar, which was bought by Pacetti.

About the same year an Englishman and a Scotchman, Thomas Jenkins and Gavin Hamilton, tried their luck in the section of the same villa called Roma Vecchia. They found a bust of Lucius Verus, another of Diocletian, a third and a fourth of two Romans, perhaps Decemviri, with the names engraved on the plinth; a life-size statue of Euterpe, two statuettes of youths playing with birds, and scenic masks; two sarcophagi, and several fragments of less importance. The best portion of these marbles was purchased by Pius VI. for the Vatican Museum, who at the same time ordered fresh excavations to be made on his own account. These excavations lasted from May 11, 1789, to May 15, 1792, and led to the discovery of the following items: Eleven statuettes belonging to the ornamentation of one or more fountains; eight life-size statues; nine heads and busts; two double herms; two sarcophagi; a mosaic pavement; several columns, pedestals, inscriptions, and other objects of interest. Carlo Torlonia purchased the grounds at the beginning of the present century, and undertook other excavations about 1828–1829, the magnificent results of which are described by Nibby[1] and by Visconti in the catalogue of the Museo Torlonia.

The last search, made by Giovanni Battista Guidi, about 1855, was also attended with considerable success. He found among other interesting things a *castellum aquae*, with its organ-like range of water-pipes, inscribed with the names of the patricians who owned property in the neighbourhood, and who drew their supply of water from this reservoir of the Villa Quintiliorum. Having myself surveyed the site of the villa on more than one occasion, I have persuaded myself that the mine is by no means exhausted.

The Villa Voconiorum was excavated at my suggestion by Signor Luigi Boccanera in 1883–1884. Its beautiful remains have since been destroyed, much against our laws, by a local owner, and its area put under cultivation. The most interesting particular gathered from these excavations is that when the statues fell, or were thrown from their pedestals, the floor of the villa was already covered with over three feet of débris. The statues therefore were still standing after the first barbarian invasions. Once for all, then, we may absolve the barbarians from the blame of a useless destruction or mutilation of classic statuary.[2]

[1] *Analisi*, Vol. III. p. 726.

[2] Gavin Hamilton excavated, in or about 1780, a round temple at the eighth mile-stone of the Appian Way, with as many statues as there were intercolumniations, each lying a few inches only from its original location. See Riccy, *Pago Lemonio*, p. 122, n. 1.

CHAPTER X

THE MONUMENTS IN THE SEVENTH CENTURY

THE early years of the seventh century were marked by three events of special significance for the history of the monuments. These are, the erection of the column of Phocas, the transformation of the Pantheon into a church, and the inauguration of the practice of transferring relics of martyrs from the Catacombs to sanctuaries within the walls.

Phocas, the murderer of the Emperor Mauritius, had seized the throne of the East in November, 602. The portraits of this "base and cowardly assassin" and of his wife Leontia were received in Rome with the customary honours by the clergy and the Senate assembled in the Basilica Julii at the Lateran, and afterward exhibited to the public in the church of S. Cesario in Palatio.[1] The Romans went even a step farther in their show of servility: they raised an honorary column, inscribed, *Phocae clementissimo principi*, in the middle of the Forum, which still remained free from the ruins that were later to bury and conceal it. This is the last monument erected in that

[1] The remains of this church are described in *Ruins and Excavations*, p. 169.

FIG. 21. — The column of Phocas in the Forum. At the right, further back, the remains of the temple of Saturn.

historical place. It marks the end of the ancient period and the beginning of the Middle Ages. "Of the three monumental columns still extant at Rome," Dyer well remarks, "two were erected to the best emperors (Trajan and Marcus Aurelius), one to the worst and basest; their merits are aptly typified by the style of their monuments."[1]

From the inscription on the pedestal of the column of Phocas (discovered February 23, 1813) we learn that the pillar was surmounted by a statue in gilt bronze. Now such a statue could not have been modelled and cast in Rome in 608 A.D. (the column was dedicated on August 1 of that year). It must have been an old statue, cast centuries before, of which, I am inclined to believe, not even the head was changed for the occasion. The column is forty-five feet high, and leans considerably toward the southeast. The style of the shaft and capital is certainly better than that prevailing in 608 A.D.; therefore, either the column was removed bodily from a classic edifice, or else the Romans and their exarch Zmaragdus dedicated to Phocas a monument which, up to his time, had borne another name.

It is interesting to note that the Forum of Trajan also was at this time free from any accumulation of rubbish. Venantius Fortunatus, a contemporary of Gregory, speaks of the custom of poets reciting in that place as still flourishing in his day (*Carm.* III. 23).

[1] *History of the City of Rome*, p. 353.

Boniface IV., elected bishop of Rome in the same year in which the column of Phocas was dedicated, obtained from that Emperor the permission to dedicate the Pantheon of Agrippa to the Virgin Mary and all Christian martyrs. This concession marks an exceedingly important moment in the history of the destruction and transformation of ancient Rome, because, as I have previously remarked, up to the beginning of the seventh century the Christians had abstained from worshipping in places where divine honours had been paid to pagan deities. No classic temple, no shrine, — only civic buildings had thus far been used for churches; but about this time all such scruples disappeared. To speak only of the edifices lining the Sacra Via and the Forum, we now find the Senate-house dedicated to St. Hadrian, the inner hall of the Augusteum to S. Maria Antiqua, the temple of Antoninus and Faustina to St. Lawrence, that of Janus to St. Dionysius, that of Saturn to the Saviour. The Heroön of Romulus, son of Maxentius, becomes the vestibule of the church of SS. Cosmas and Damianus; a chapel to St. Peter is raised in the vestibule of the temple of Venus and Rome; another to S. Martina in the *Secretarium Senatus;* a third to SS. Sergius and Bacchus, near the steps of the temple of Concord; and a fourth to an unknown saint in the Basilica of Constantine.[1]

[1] Cf. *Pagan and Christian Rome*, p. 162.

It would be interesting to know whether the Pantheon was submitted to any alteration in the process of transformation into a church. Were the colossal portrait statues of Augustus and Agrippa still standing, in the year 608, in their niches under the portico, or those of the ancestral gods of the Julian gens in their shrines under the dome? Were the great rosettes of gilt bronze still fixed in the coffers of the dome itself, and the bronze bas-reliefs still ornamenting the pediment of the pronaos? It is difficult to give a satisfactory answer to these queries. I incline to the view that when the Pantheon was placed under the protection of the Queen of Martyrs, it was already reduced to the present state, or rather to the state in which it was before the spoliations of Constans II. in 663, of Urban VIII. in 1625, and of Benedict XIV. in 1747.[1] In the lapse of time between the closing of temples and the abandonment of the public baths, and the reign of Phocas, the statues of the gods and heroes must have been removed or thrown off from their pedestals,[2] and the rosettes of the dome probably

[1] Constans II. stole the tiles of gilded bronze which covered the roof of the pronaos and the dome; Urban VIII. melted into cannon 410,778 pounds of metal from the trusses of the pronaos; and Benedict XIV. destroyed the marble veneering of the attic story.

[2] For the fate of the three Caryatides by Diogenes the Athenian, formerly in the Paganica and Giustiniani palaces, supposed to have formed a part of the decoration of the attic, see *Notizie degli scavi*, 1881, pp. 265-267; Emil Braun, *Bull. Inst.*, 1853, p. 36.

had fallen, one by one, through the disintegration of the masonry of the coffers. The bas-reliefs of the pediment had perhaps escaped spoliation. It seems that when the Piazza della Rotonda was first excavated and paved by Pope Eugenius IV. (1431-1439), a head, possibly of Agrippa, the leg of a horse, and the wheel of a chariot, all cast in bronze, were found at the foot of the steps. These fragments may have fallen from the pediment. No mention is made of marble statues, except of a head attributed to Cybele, which Camillo Fanucci claims to have seen lying on the floor near the high altar in the year 1600.[1]

Another clew as to the state of the Pantheon, when taken possession of by the Church, is given by the clumsy restorations made by Boniface IV. (610 A.D.), by Vitalianus (663), and Gregory III. (735), with materials taken from other edifices, such as the marble slab containing the honorary inscription of Lucius Albinus, removed from the Forum of Augustus (*C. I. L.* I. 285), the beautiful frieze from the temple of Isis (illustrated by Visconti in *Bull. Com.* Vol. IV., 1876, p. 92), and other such spoils. Even more important is the fact that some of these spoils belonged to the Pantheon itself, as the two beautiful friezes, with festoons and candelabras and sacred implements, removed from the sides of the great door, and the doorpost taken from one of the side entrances.

[1] Camillo Fanucci, *Trattato di tutte l' opere pie*, etc., c. xxxvi.

FIG. 22. — The Pronaos of the Pantheon.

These three pieces had been used in the restoration of the steps leading from the square in front of the Pantheon to the pronaos (Fig. 22), and were found between December, 1874, and September, 1875.

The designation of S. Maria ad Martyres, given to the Pantheon by Boniface IV., recalls an interesting fact. According to the *Liber Pontificalis*, this name was given to the newly consecrated church on account of twenty-eight cartloads of sacred bones which had been removed from the Catacombs and placed in a basin of porphyry under the high altar. This was the beginning of an important change.

I have stated above that burial in the Catacombs was given up in 410, the year of the storming of Rome by Alaric, and that great damage was done to them in 537, during the siege of Vitiges. As the country around Rome became more and more insecure and unhealthy, and was almost completely abandoned by its inhabitants at the time of the Langobardic inroads, it was deemed necessary to place within the protection of the city walls the bones of the martyrs, whose tombs, from the time of Constantine, had more and more become centres of pilgrimage. The first translation of remains is the one just mentioned, of the time of Boniface IV.; the second took place in 648; the third in 682, when the bodies of Primus and Felicianus were removed from Nomentum, and those of Viatrix, Faustinus, and Simplicius from the cemetery of Generosa, at the sixth mile-stone of the Via Campana, in the Vigna Ceccarelli, near La Magliana.

The last exploiting of the Catacombs for the bones of martyrs was due to Paschal I. (817–824). Contemporary documents speak of "innumerable" transferences of relics. One of them,—the official register of the relics, removed July 20, 817, to S. Prassede,—mentions twenty-three hundred bodies deposited under the chapel of S. Zeno, which Paschal I. had built in memory of his mother, Theodora Episcopa. The mosaic legend of the apse of St. Caecilia speaks likewise of the removal of bodies *quae primum in cryptis pausabant*.

These removals of relics are interesting from another point of view,—they mark the beginning of archaeological research among the remains of the great imperial thermae. The relics of martyrs were, as a rule, deposited in basins and bath-tubs of rare marble, in which the thermae of Caracalla and Diocletian particularly abounded. The bones of Viatrix, Faustinus, and Simplicius, mentioned above, were placed by Leo II. under the high altar of the church of S. Vibiana "in a basin of oriental alabaster of oval shape, twenty-five palms in circumference, with heads of leopards in high relief." Stephen V., while rebuilding the church of SS. Apostoli in 816 A.D., likewise placed the bodies of Eugenia and Claudia "in a basin of porphyry" (*in concha porphyretica*). Two archaeologists, Giovanni

Marangoni and Francesco de Ficoroni, have made a list, interesting though incomplete, of these precious spoils of Roman baths used in churches; to it we should add another class of works of art similarly employed, the sarcophagi, which occasionally take the place of the bath basins, in spite of their reliefs of a distinctly pagan character.

Singular as this practice seems to us, we cannot judge of the taste of the Roman clergy in those dark and semi-barbaric days in the light of our own feelings and education. They could hardly spell the Latin words inscribed on the marble slabs which they used in the pavements, in the walls, and in the altars of their churches; much less could they understand their meaning. A pedestal covered with symbols of the worship of the Magna Mater, in its most crude and hateful form, was used as an altar of the Crucifix in the church of S. Michele in Borgo. The tombstone of Flavius Agricola from Tibur, with its epicurean legend, was discovered August 14, 1626, a few feet from the grave of St. Peter, in the foundations of the left front column of the Baldacchino. The high altar in the church of S. Teodoro was supported, until 1703, by a round altar, on the rim of which the following words were inscribed: "On this marble of the gentiles incense was offered to the gods." The pavement of St. Paul's without the walls was patched with 931 miscellaneous inscriptions.

A worshipper raising his eyes toward the apse of the church of SS. Cosmas and Damianus, could behold at the same time the great mosaic figure of the Saviour, and a group of the twin founders of the City sucking the wolf, in *opus sectile*. In the basilica of Junius Bassus on the Esquiline, Christianised under the name of St. Andrew at the Manger, he could see the group of the Saviour with the Apostle in the Tribune, and, turning to the side walls, the portraits of Nero, Galba, and six other emperors, Diana hunting the stag, Hylas stolen by the Nymphs, Cybele on the chariot drawn by lions, the chariot of Apollo, initiates performing mysterious Egyptian rites, and other representations from pagan cults. I may mention in the last instance the church of S. Martina, formerly the Secretarium Senatus, the walls of which were adorned with the bas-reliefs from the arch of Marcus Aurelius, representing the Emperor sacrificing before the altar of Jupiter Optimus Maximus.

The Epitome of the Chronicon Cassinense, which dates from the time of Stephen II. (752–757), says that after the "recovery of the Cross" made by Heraclius in 629, the Emperor betook himself to Rome, where he was proclaimed Emperor, and given the imperial diadem in the throne room of the palace of the Caesars (*in augustali solio Caesareani Palatii a senatoribus positus et diademate redimitus, monocrator constitutus est*). This passage of the Chronicon shows that the palace, in spite of the pillages of Totila, of Genseric, and of the Romans themselves, could still be used for state ceremonies in the first half of the seventh century.

By palace I mean the special wing known in classical times by the name of "Domitian's house" (οἰκία Δομιτιανοῦ) or *Aedes publicae populi Romani*. This great structure had never been used as a dwelling by the emperors, but simply as a state residence where they held their levees, delivered their decisions, presided over councils of state, received foreign envoys, and gave official banquets. The building had never required repairs, on account of the enormous solidity of its construction. The remains of the hall, where the coronation of Heraclius took place, are still to be seen. It was excavated by Bianchini in 1724, and again by Rosa in 1865. Judging from the finds made on these two occasions, there is no doubt that in 629 this throne room was well preserved, not only in its essential parts, such as walls, ceiling, roof, and windows, but also in its decorative details. Bianchini discovered two columns of giallo antico which stood on either side of the main door, which were sold by the Duke of Parma to the stone-cutters Perini and Macinocchi for 3000 scudi; a threshold made of a block of Greek marble so large that the high altar of the church of the Rotonda has since been cut out of it; fragments of the sixteen columns of pavonazzetto supporting the entablature, with capitals and bases exquisitely cut in ivory-coloured marble, and two out of the eight colossal statues which stood in the niches. If so much remained of the decoration of the hall in 1724, after it had been at the mercy of lime-burners and stone-cutters for the space of ten centuries, the hall itself may well have been in almost perfect condition at the time of the coronation of Heraclius.

Another wing of the palace, the northeast section of the *Domus Gaiana*, which overlooks the Forum and the Sacra Via, seems to have been kept in repair and sometimes occupied by the popes, as a practical evidence of their political power in Rome. This wing was put under the care of an officer styled *a cura Palatii*. About 680 one of these officers, named Plato, rebuilt or repaired the long staircase which ascends from the Clivus Victoriae to the rooms above. His son, having been elected pope in 705 under the name of John VII., conceived the plan of making the Domus Gaiana the official residence of the bishops of Rome, above the present church of S. Maria Liberatrice (*super ecclesiam sanctae Dei genetricis quae antiqua vocatur episcopium construere voluit*).

John VII. did not live to see his project carried out; as his successors took no interest in it, they repaired to the monasteries and strongholds of the Palatine only in case of necessity. There were four of these ecclesiastical establishments on the Palatine, the Ecclesia and Monasterium S. Caesarii in Palatio, first mentioned in the time of Phocas, 603 A.D., but probably older, where the images of the Byzantine emperors were exhibited to the public as a symbol of the power that they still claimed over Rome; the monastery called Palladium, now represented by the church of S. Sebastiano alla Polveriera in the Vigna Barberini, near the east corner of the hill, a strongly fortified place where the popes sought refuge and protection in times of popular outbreaks; the Turris Cartularia built on the platform of the temple of Jupiter Stator, by the arch of Titus, in which the archives of the church were kept for many centuries; and lastly the Septizonium, the greatest mediaeval stronghold of the Palatine, garrisoned by the Frangipanis under the ownership of the abbots of the monastery SS. Andreae et Gregorii ad Clivum Scauri.

The latest bit of evidence regarding the real or nominal occupancy of the Palatine episcopal residence by the popes came to light November 8, 1883, during the excavation of the House of the Vestals. At the northeast corner of the peristyle the remains of a modest mediaeval dwelling were discovered, belonging to a high official of the court of Marinus II., — a pontiff, otherwise obscure, who occupied the chair of St. Peter from 942 to 946. This official must have been in charge of the pope's rooms which were placed among the ruins of the Domus Gaiana. It is important to notice that when this small house was built, at the beginning of the tenth century, the pavement of the Atrium Vestae was already covered with a layer of rubbish five feet thick. The columns of the peristyle had been removed or knocked down from their bases, the walls stripped of their marble veneering, and even the small tesserae of the mosaic pavement wrenched from their setting. Around the Palatine hill clustered the Byzantine colony, to which we owe the construction of the churches of the Anastasis, of S. Maria in Schola Graeca, of S. Saba, of St. Theodore, and of St. George, still existing, as well as those of S. Euplos and S. Phocas, which have long since disappeared.[1]

The visit of Heraclius to Rome in 629 is connected with another event in the history of the destruction of the City. He made a present to Pope Honorius I. (625-640) of the gilt-bronze tiles which covered the roof of the temple of Venus and Rome, to be removed to that of St. Peter's. This fact proves that the temple was at that time in a good state of repair; while, on the other hand, the stripping off of the tiles was a sure way to promote the downfall of the building. Specimens of these tiles were seen and described by Justus Rycq and Giacomo Grimaldi at the time of Paul V., who destroyed, in 1606, the roof and the nave of old St. Peter's.

Another famous edifice fell at the same time into the

[1] For further particulars, see the interesting chapter on the history of the Palatine in Grisar's *History of the Popes in the Middle Ages*.

hands of the Pope, the Curia or Senate-house, which he dedicated to St. Hadrian, a saint otherwise unknown. The ancient decorations of the hall, the gilt coffers of the vaulted roof, the marble panelling of the walls, the bas-reliefs of the pediment, and the bronze door did not suffer damage or alteration with the "Christianisation" of the building. They disappeared partly in 1589, partly in 1654, at the hands of Cardinal Agostino Cusano and of Alfonso Sotomayor, who raised the floor of the church to the modern level, and altered the classic shape of the building. The bronze doors were removed to the church of St. John Lateran by Alexander VII., but as the folds, which filled an aperture about eighteen by eleven feet, were smaller than the doorway of the Lateran, a band, ornamented with the typical stars of the Pope (Chigi), was added to the ancient metal work. A third edifice, the Heroön of Romulus, son of Maxentius, lost the bronze tiles of its roof about the same time. Pope Sergius I. saved the temple from destruction by covering the dome with sheets of lead.[1]

On July 5, 663, Rome had for the last time the misfortune of an imperial visit. Constans II., compelled by a guilty conscience on account of a fratricide to

[1] See De Rossi, *Bull. di arch. crist.*, 1867, p. 62. The sheets of lead were afterward stolen, and vegetation, of considerable growth, sprung up on the bare dome. When the monument was restored, in 1879, I found roots of ilexes, and fig-trees, four inches in diameter, wedged in the cracks of the masonry.

wander from sanctuary to sanctuary, had undertaken a pilgrimage to Rome in the spring of that year, and was met by Pope Vitalianus and the few inhabitants near the sixth mile-stone of the Appian Way. The short and friendly visit of this Christian emperor proved most disastrous to the Roman monuments; he seized everything of value which, after the repeated sieges of Vandals, Goths, and Lombards, had been left to plunder. The statement of Dyer in regard to this robbery is not exaggerated. "In the twelve days which Constans spent at Rome," says this writer, "he carried off as many bronze statues as he could lay hands on; and though the Pantheon seemed to possess a double claim to protection, as having been presented by Phocas to the Pope, and as having been converted into a Christian church, yet Constans was mean and sacrilegious enough to carry off the tiles of gilt bronze which covered it. After perpetrating these acts, which were, at least, as bad as robberies, and attending mass at the tomb of St. Peter, Constans carried off his booty to Syracuse. His plunder ultimately fell into the hands of the Saracens."

A remarkable discovery has been made in later years bearing on this visit of Constans to Rome. The Emperor, between his acts of doubtful devotion in churches and basilicas, found time to visit the pagan monuments and ruins. These visits were recorded by one of his attendants by scratching his sovereign's name on a prominent part of every building which the party dishonoured with its presence. One of these *graffiti* is to be found on the four-faced arch, Janus Quadrifrons, on the right side of the archway facing the church of S. Giorgio in Velabro, the ancient Forum Boarium; another on the very top of Trajan's column.

Possibly more than mere records of a visit of curiosity, these scratchings are records of plunder. There is every probability that the statue of the "best of Princes," on the top of the column of Trajan, was carried off by this visitor. The fate of the statue on the column of Marcus Aurelius also is not known; perhaps it was hurled down from the top of the column, and broken into pieces by the fall. When the Marchese Ferrajuoli rebuilt the foundations of his palace on the south side of the Piazza Colonna, in 1868, the finger of the left hand of a bronze statue of colossal size was discovered in the layer of rubbish which covers the ancient stone pavement of the square. It is quite possible that a careful examination of the principal Roman monuments, such as the Coliseum, Pantheon, and the column of Marcus Aurelius, would lead to the discovery of other graffiti of a similar character, and thus enable us to follow, step by step, the wanderings of the last Emperor who saw Rome before the ravages of the Normans.

CHAPTER XI

THE INCURSION OF THE SARACENS, IN 846, AND THE EXTENSION OF THE FORTIFICATIONS OF THE CITY

THE conquest of Palermo by the Saracens in 831 caused the reigning Pope, Gregory IV., to adopt certain measures of defence. The first was the construction of a fort as an outpost at the mouth of the Tiber; another was the abandonment of the churches outside the walls, in the wilderness of the Campagna, their contents being transferred within the shelter of the City's defences.

The founding of Gregoriopolis, the fortress at the mouth of the river, is described in the *Liber Pontificalis*.[1] We are informed that the ancient colony and harbour of Ostia, "stricken with age, seemed to have been altogether destroyed"; yet there were a few fever-stricken inhabitants still wandering among the ruins. Gregory is praised by the biographer as having built a new line of walls with portcullis gates, crowned with powerful batteries (*petrariae*), and protected by a deep moat. The account is greatly exaggerated, to judge from the remains of this Gregoriopolis which

[1] Gregorius, IV. 38.

the late Carlo Ludovico Visconti and I laid bare in the winter of 1867-1868. What Gregory IV. or his representatives actually did at Ostia in the way of erecting fortifications amounts to little or nothing. They simply selected two or three blocks of old houses on the left side of the main street and filled up the doors, windows, and shop-fronts with mud walls. They also barricaded the openings of the streets which ran between the blocks. It is possible, although we found no evidence, that the houses surrounding this rudimentary fort on the opposite sides of the boundary streets were levelled to the ground.

The Saracenic invasion of 846 is a well-known event in its main lines, but very uncertain in its details. The biographer of Sergius II. (844-847), a contemporary, and perhaps an eye-witness, of the facts, leaves off his description at the most critical point. It seems that on the 10th of August, 846, Count Adalbert, Governor of Tuscany and protector of Corsica, sent warning that a fleet of seventy-three Saracenic vessels, carrying eleven thousand men and five hundred horses, had been signalled making for the mouth of the Tiber. Count Adalbert urged the Romans to place within the protection of the walls the bodies of the princes of the apostles, Peter and Paul, as well as the great treasure in gold and silver which many generations of pilgrims had deposited over their tombs in the outlying and defenceless basilicas of the Via Cornelia and of the

Via Ostiensis. The Romans, however, paid little attention to the warning of Adalbert, but satisfied themselves with communicating the contents of his letter to the villagers and farmers of the Campagna, that these might assemble for the defence of the coast. Villagers and farmers, likewise, treated the message with contempt; so that when the Saracens landed at the mouth of the Tiber, on the twenty-third of the month, they found Gregoriopolis abandoned, and were able to make that outpost their base of operations.

In these straits the Romans showed as much weakness, not to call it cowardice, as they had previously shown want of forethought. The only inhabitants who had sufficient courage to rush to the defence of Porto (on the side of the river opposite Ostia, and connected with it by means of a "wretched bridge") were the members of the foreign colony, the Saxons, the Frisians, and the Franks, who lived in the quarter called Burgus, between the castle of S. Angelo and the Vatican.

After two encounters, in which nineteen skirmishers lost their lives, Porto was taken by the infidels and the garrison put to the sword; the few survivors were pursued as far as Ponte Galera. This happened on the 26th of August; on the following day the Saracens marched upon Rome, while their fleet was towed upstream, and took possession — free and undisturbed — of the basilicas of St. Peter and St. Paul outside the walls.

I have taken the pains to estimate — on the authority of the *Liber Pontificalis* — the weight of gold and silver lavished on the rich decorations of the two churches from the time of Constantine down; as nearly as I can reckon it, about three tons of gold and thirty of silver must have fallen into the hands of the Saracens, — an almost fabulous booty, which well repaid them for the cost and trouble of their expedition.

While these depredations were going on, the Romans attempted a sally in the "plains of Nero" (the Prati di Castello), but were easily driven back. The farmers of the Campagna, supported by the villagers from the Alban and Tiburtine hills, seem to have been more successful in attacking and dispersing a band of pirates near the Basilica of St. Paul. For this reason, or perhaps because they had secured more booty than their vessels would hold, the invaders began their retreat, after slaughtering a great number of men, destroying by fire many towns and strongholds, and carrying off "a very great booty of people and of all things." Their infantry and cavalry went south along the Appian Way, while the fleet skirted the coast as far as Gaeta. Fleet and crews were ultimately lost in a gale off the coast of Sicily.

The most important circumstance in this chain of events is the fate of the tombs of St. Peter and St. Paul. There can be no doubt that the Romans despised the warning of Count Adalbert in regard to the safety of the treasures in gold and silver belonging to both these tombs; all the accounts agree in testifying that the Saracens seized in either place *innumerabilia bona*. Did the people of Rome heed the second part of the admonition as regards the bodies of the apostles? Did they open the sarcophagi and carry the precious contents within the City walls?

The answer is more than doubtful. Pope Sergius, in the first place, was so broken down by gout and *humor podagricus* that he could attend to no duties; he was "good for nothing," according to the statement of his own biographer. His brother, Benedict, we learn from the same source, was "extremely dull and passive" (*brutus et stolidus valde*), and so of even less account. In the second place, the Saracens fell on both sanctuaries like a thunderbolt, according to a plan of campaign that had been carefully matured beforehand.

What this plan of the Moslem invaders was, it is easy to understand. Suppose that the crusaders had taken possession of Mecca. Would not their first aim have been to invade the Kasbah and scatter to the four winds the bones of the prophet? A like policy seems to have been followed by the infidels in regard to our sanctuaries. They certainly entered and plundered the treasures of the crypt "where reposed the most holy body of the Prince of the Apostles" (*ubi sacratissimum corpus principis apostolorum requiescit*); here is the proof of it. Leo III. had placed over the tomb a bas-relief of gilt silver, representing the Redeemer, the Virgin Mary, Peter, Paul, Andrew, and Petronilla. The bas-relief was stolen by the Saracens, and a copy was substituted in its place by Leo IV. after the retreat of the invaders.

It would be impossible to discuss in a book like the present all the arguments brought forward to prove or to deny the profanation of the sanctuaries of both Peter and Paul in 846. My opinion is that the fate of the two holy places was not in all respects the same; that the sarcophagus of St. Peter, placed in a subterranean crypt and protected by a case of solid metal embedded in masonry, escaped rifling, while that of St. Paul, a plain marble coffin level with the floor of the basilica, was certainly injured or destroyed. We find the evidence of the fact last mentioned in the life of Benedict III.:[1] *Sepulchrum (Pauli apostoli) quod a Sarracenis destructum fuerat, perornavit.* The word *destructum*, however, cannot be taken in a literal sense; the lid of the sarcophagus, with the epitaph PAULO APOSTOLO MART(YRI) engraved in the style of the age of Constantine, is still in existence. I saw it on Decem-

---

[1] Chapter xxii. in Duchesne's edition of the *Liber Pontificalis*, Vol. II. p. 145. The passage relating to St. Peter's, in the life of Leo IV., mentions not the grave, but the altar of the Apostle as having been injured by the Saracens: *beatiss. Petri altare violatum et ad vilitatem perductum.*

ber 1, 1891, having lowered myself from the fenestella under the high altar.[1] (Fig. 23.)

The most noteworthy consequence of these events, from a topographical point of view, was the inclusion

Fig. 23. — The tomb of St. Paul and the canopy of Arnolfo di Lapo in S. Paolo fuori le Mura, after the fire of 1823.

of the Vatican district in the City proper, and the construction of two powerful outlying forts, one at St. Paul's, the other at the church of S. Lorenzo fuori le Mura.

The walls of the Civitas Leonina, or Burgus, are

[1] See *Pagan and Christian Rome*, p. 157.

still in existence, and are properly considered a masterpiece of mediaeval military engineering. Leo IV. undertook to imitate, to a certain extent, the construction of the wall of Aurelian. His structure is twelve feet thick, and has two galleries, one above the other. The lower gallery is supported by open arcades facing within. The upper one is level with the battlements. The arcades of the lower gallery were walled up in the fifteenth century by Pope Borgia, and the gallery itself transformed into a secret passage — the famous Corridojo di Castello — connecting the palace of the Vatican with the fortress of S. Angelo. To this corridor many popes and cardinals have been indebted for escape from death or servitude; one of the most striking instances is that of Pope Clement VII., who in May, 1527, fled through this passage from the hordes of Charles of Bourbon.

The construction of the Leonine wall, so elaborate in the level stretch between the Vatican and the fortress of S. Angelo, becomes more simple on the hill behind the church, the steep slopes of which constitute a natural and effective line of defence. Here we find a plain wall with no galleries, save a passage at the height of the battlements, as may be seen in our illustration. (Fig. 24.) The most exposed angles were protected by round towers, two of which are still in existence and form a conspicuous landmark in the Vatican landscape. The one represented in the illustration, which stands at a height of 187 feet above the sea, commands an unlimited view over the Campagna and the coast, and is therefore described as the

FIG. 24.— Tower of the wall of Leo IV., now used as an observatory.

turris unde mare prospicitur in the early representations of the Vatican group. It is now used as an observatory for photographing the section of the heavens which was allotted to the Holy See by the International Astronomical Congress.[1] The other tower is used as a chapel for the new summer casino of Leo XIII.

The pontifical treasury and the resources of the citizens of Rome were unequal to the task of completing the walls in the required time. A system of forced service (*praestatio operis*) was in consequence resorted to, and the colonists of the fortified farms of the Campagna were called upon to take a share in the work. Two inscriptions, now affixed to the arch which spans the Via Angelica, give important details of the scheme adopted to obtain thus speedy assistance and cheap labour. One says, "In the time of our Lord the Pope Leo IV., the Militia Saltisina (a colony on the road to Ardea, fifteen miles from Rome) built these two towers, and the wall between them;" the other, "In the time of our Lord the Pope Leo IV., the Militia Capracorum (a colony founded by Hadrian I. near the ruins of Veii on the site of the present farm of S. Cornelia) built this tower and the wall which connects it with the next." Both companies declare that they worked under the direction of a certain Agatho, who was probably the chief engineer of the Leonine wall.

In 880 John VIII. did for St. Paul's without the Walls what Leo IV. had done thirty years before for St. Peter's, but with this difference, that while the

[1] This work is entrusted mostly to Cavaliere Mannucci, to whom I am indebted for the illustration.

Burgus was included in and became a part of the City proper, the Basilica Ostiensis with its adjoining monastery and hospices remained a detached fort, connected with the City only by means of a colonnade a mile long. The stronghold — of which no trace is now to be seen above ground — was named Johannipolis after its founder. A second detached fort was built about the same time for the protection of the basilica of S. Lorenzo fuori le Mura. No historical document mentions the fact, but we possess a drawing of Martin Heemskerk which shows the state of the stronghold about 1534.[1] The fact that two inhabited centres of the Campagna, Saltisinum and Capracorum, could furnish a strong contingent of soldier-workmen for the defence of the Capital, seems to prove that a few fortified farms did escape from the depredation of the Saracens. I may add that some of the Saracens themselves, namely, the prisoners taken at St. Paul's and on the road to Gaeta, were compelled to take a share in the work, the fact being recorded in an inscription.[2]

The extent of the zone plundered in the fearful visitation of 846 can be determined with the help of the list of churches which Leo IV. had to refurnish with sacred implements and vestments. None of the church buildings, however, seem to have been materially damaged; at least I have not been able to find in the *Liber Pon-*

[1] Reproduced in *Ruins and Excavations*, Fig. 35.
[2] De Rossi, *Inscriptiones Christianae urbis Romae*, Vol. II. p. 347.

tificalis any mention of Leo IV. or his successors having repaired roofs, walls, windows, or doors. The list of plundered churches comprises those of Silva Candida, of the delta of the Tiber, of Ostia and Porto. I must record especially that of S. Cyriacus on the Via Ostiensis, because it was just in the neighbourhood of its remains that Signor Pietro Rocchi discovered some twenty-five years ago traces of one of the Saracenic camps, consisting mainly of daggers and poniards with curved blades of Oriental make. Other churches are mentioned on the Tusculan and Alban hills (Frascati, Morena, Massa Maruli), and along the Via Appia as far as Terracina and Fondi. Important, above all, is the mention of the church of SS. Cosmas and Damianus (S. Cosimato) near Subiaco, because it shows that the Saracens carried their devastation as far as the upper valley of the Anio, and into the very heart of the Simbruine Mountains.

We find a survival from this incursion at the present day in the village of *Saracinesco*, perched like an eagle's nest on a conical and almost inaccessible peak at a height of 2500 feet above the sea, and of 1350 feet above S. Cosimato. There is no doubt that a foraging party, having been cut off from the main body, and finding a retreat impossible, took shelter among these rocky precipices, and that afterwards they were allowed to form a settlement and live in peace by substituting the cross for the crescent. Some of the inhabitants, who come to Rome every winter clad in their picturesque costumes as painters' models, have preserved their Arabic names, like El-Mansour (Almansorre). Elmansour is also the name of a cave in the neighbourhood of the village. From this point of view, therefore, our valley of the Anio forms a counterpart of the Saas-Thal in the Valaisan Alps, the villages and peaks of which still preserve their Saracenic names (Monte Moro, Allalin, Mischabel, Alphubel, Almagell, Balferin, etc.), from the invasion of 927.

CHAPTER XII

THE FLOOD OF 856

ON January 6, 856, when Benedict III. was pope, the Tiber rose violently, broke through the embankments, and flooded the lower quarters of the City to the depth of several feet. According to the *Liber Pontificalis* the waters reached the highest step of the stairs of St. Dionysius, near the present church of S. Silvestro in Capite, and the architrave of the door of S. Maria in Via Lata. Houses fell or were washed away by the hundred, trees were uprooted, men and cattle drowned, and crops destroyed, all the way down the river from Rome to the sea.

What damage was in this instance done to the classic monuments we do not know; but the records show that during the Middle Ages there were several destructive inundations of the Tiber, and they are described with an almost stereotyped formula in the *Liber Pontificalis*. The formula runs thus: —

On such an hour, on such a day of such a year,[1] the waters broke through the *posterula* of St. Agatha, and

[1] *Hora diei X.* for the inundation of October 30, 860. See *Liber Pontificalis*, Vol. II. p. 145, chap. xxiii.

rushing over the waste fields of the Campus Martius, followed the line of the Via Flaminia (the modern Corso) to the foot of the Capitoline hill; then, pushed back by this obstacle, they followed the line of the Pallacinae, etc.

Such a description would not be applied to a gentle rising of the waters, which quietly spread over the low-

FIG. 25. — The Forum flooded by the Tiber — 1898.

lying districts, giving time to the citizens to save life and property; we have here rather a sudden outburst, produced by the breaking away of an obstacle, whether a levee, or an embankment, or a wall. In the inundation of 856 the obstacle must have been in the line of the walls of Aurelian and Honorius, which followed the left bank of the river from the *Turris ubi umbra Neronis diu mansitavit*, by the present Ponte Margherita, to the Ponte Sisto. There were two or three gaps in the wall, called *posterulae*, which served to give access to the ferries and to the mooring stations along the bank. The *posterula* of St. Agatha, through which the inundations broke, was the northernmost of the gaps, and consequently the most exposed of all; any temporary obstruction of the water here would be apt to give way first under the pressure of the flood.

Even in modern times floods have been not infrequent. Our illustration shows the Forum under water at the time of a freshet (Fig. 25). A destructive inundation in 1557 carried away part of the Pons Aemilius (Fig. 44).

CHAPTER XIII

THE ROME OF THE EINSIEDLEN ITINERARY

THE name *Einsiedlen Itinerary* has been given to a summary description of Rome dating from the ninth century, which is appended to a collection of inscriptions, mostly of Roman origin, in a manuscript volume formerly in the library of the Abbey of Pfeffers, now in that of Einsiedeln, in Switzerland. The volume has been examined and illustrated in its minutest details by Haenel, Jordan, De Rossi, and myself.[1] Our joint researches have proved that the *Itinerary* was made up of the legends of a map of Rome of the time of Charlemagne, prepared for the use of pilgrims. The legends, therefore, are arranged so as to form eleven itineraries, or routes, between the main centres of religious attraction. The list is as follows: —

ROUTE
  I. From the Aelian Bridge to the Esquiline, by S. Lucia in Selce.
  II. From the Aelian Bridge to the Porta Salaria.

[1] Haenel, in *Archiv für Philologie und Pädagogik*, Vol. V. (1837) pp. 115–138; Jordan, *Topographie von Rom*, Vol. II. p. 329; De Rossi, *Inscr. Christ.*, Vol. II. pp. 9 *et seq.*; Lanciani, *l' Itinerario di Einsiedlen e l' Ordo di Benedetto Canonico*, Rome, 1891.

THE ROME OF THE EINSIEDLEN ITINERARY

III. From the Aelian Bridge to the Porta Asinaria (now S. Giovanni).
IV. From the Aelian Bridge to St. Paul's without the Walls.
V. From the Porta Nomentana to the Forum Romanum.
VI. From the Porta Flaminia (now Porta del Popolo) to the Capitol (Via di Marforio).
VII. From the Porta Tiburtina (S. Lorenzo) to the Subura by the Esquiline gate of Servius; and again
VIII. From the Porta Tiburtina to the Subura by the Viminal gate of Servius.
IX. From the Porta Aurelia (S. Pancrazio) to the Porta Praenestina (now Porta Maggiore).
X. From the Circus Maximus to the Porta Metroni, across the Caelian Hill.
XI. From the Porta Appia (now Porta di S. Sebastiano) to the Schola Graeca (Bocca della Verità).

The Ninth Route, from west to east, marks what the camp surveyors would call the *decumanus maior;* the Third, from north to south, approximately, gives us the line of a *cardo*, at right angles with it; the others are designed to illustrate the four quarters formed by the intersection of the *cardo* and the *decumanus*. The author of the document had two purposes in view: first, to show the pilgrims their way from one basilica to another, from the grave of one martyr to that of another; and secondly, to point out to them the most conspicuous edifices, profane as well as sacred, which they would see on the right or on the left of their path. The map used by the compiler of the *Itinerary* is the oldest of which we have knowledge, after those of the time of Constantine, which served for the compilation of the *Notitia* and of the *Curiosum Urbis;* in fact, I believe it to be a revised edition of the Constantinian map, because some of the names are so distinctly classical (as, Vicus Patricii, Minervium, Hadrianum) as to betray a much earlier origin than the time of Charlemagne.

The streets along which the pilgrim is led through the City are exactly those of imperial Rome; no change had yet taken place in their direction, and their pavement of blocks of basalt, worn by age, was not yet covered with a layer of rubbish or with sand from the inundations of the Tiber. I am speaking, of course, in general; for there is more than one instance of deviation from a straight line, in order to avoid obstacles placed in the way by the downfall of some great building of the Republic or of the Empire.

A conception of the importance of this document, as throwing light on the state of the Roman monuments in the ninth century, may be gained from the first of the Routes, which takes us from the Aelian Bridge to the Esquiline, directly through the heart of the City. The edifices are grouped in three columns: those on the right of the path, IN D(*extra*); those on the left, IN S(*inistra*); and those crossed by the path itself. The text says: —

THE ROME OF THE EINSIEDLEN ITINERARY 145

FROM THE GATE OF ST. PETER TO THE CHURCH OF
S. LUCIA IN ORTHEA

On the Right	*On the Left*
The Circus Flaminius.	The church of S. Laurentius in Damaso.
The Rotunda.	The theatre of Pompey. The Cypress.
The thermae of Commodus.	The church of St. Lawrence. The Capitol.
The Forum of Trajan and its column.	The church of S. Sergius, where is the Umbilicus Romae.
The Arch of Septimius Severus.	
The Tiber.	The equestrian statue of Constantine.
The church of St. Hadrian.	
The Forum Romanum.	
The church of St. Agatha.	
Subura.	
The thermae of Constantine.	The church of S. Pudens in Vico Patricii.
The church of S. Vitalis in Vico Longo, where the beautiful horses are.	The church of S. Laurentius in Formoso. Back again by the Subura.
The church of S. Euphemia in Vico Patricii.	The thermae of Trajan ad Vincula.

The gate of St. Peter, from which we start, is the gate of the Aurelian wall, which opened at the left or Cistiberine entrance to the Aelian Bridge, on the site of the present Piazza di Ponte S. Angelo. Its classical name of Porta Aurelia (nova) had since the time of Procopius (*Goth.* I. 19) been superseded by that of Peter, "the chief of the apostles." We now enter the

Via del Banco di S. Spirito, Via dei Banchi Vecchi, and Via del Pellegrino, all ancient as shown by the remains of Roman basaltic pavement which are constantly discovered under the modern pavement at a depth varying from ten to fifteen feet. The buildings pointed out on the left are: the Stadium, where now is the Piazza Navona, to which the name of Circus Flaminius is wrongly applied; the Rotunda, or Pantheon; the Thermae Commodianae, probably the Baths of Agrippa restored by Commodus. First on the right are the Library and archives of the Church of Rome, founded by Pope Damasus in the barracks of the green squadron of charioteers (Stabula Factionis Prasinae, S. Laurentius in Prasino); and the theatre of Pompey, the remains of which occupy the space between the Piazza di Campo di Fiori and the Via Argentina.

We are not sure what is meant by "the Cypress" (*Cupressus*), which in our itinerary follows the mention of Pompey's theatre. Names of streets, or even of quarters, derived from a solitary tree growing conspicuously in a wilderness of ruins, are not infrequent in Rome. Our Ninth Ward (Rione) is actually called della Pigna, "Pine-tree Ward"; we have also a Piazza dell' Olmo, "Elm-tree Square," and a Piazzetta del Fico, "Fig-tree"; a Via dell' Arancio, etc. Yet, while such designations may be adopted by the populace, it seems hardly credible that they should have been registered in such a document as the *Itinerary*, and put down as indicating one of the most important landmarks of the City.

Resuming our journey toward the Forum, we enter the Via delle Botteghe Oscure, skirting the east side of the Circus Flaminius (the site of which is indicated by that of the church of S. Laurentius in Pensilis, built among and above its ruins), then the Via di S. Marco or Pallacinae, and lastly the Via di Marforio, named Clivus Argentarius in antiquity, and Ascesa Prothi in the Middle Ages. The *Itinerary* mentions the Capitoline hill and the church of SS. Sergius and Bacchus on the left, the Forum and the column of Trajan on the right. Entering the Forum Romanum by the arch of Septimius Severus, we turn at once to the left, and following the succession of short streets, Via della Croce Bianca, de' Monti, Leonina, and Via di S. Lucia in Selce, corresponding to the Argiletum, Subura, and to the Clivus Suburanus, we reach the end of the journey at the Esquiline gate, in the neighbourhood of the church of S. Lucia in Orthea, better known under the name of S. Lucia in Selce.

Nine points of interest are recorded on the left, namely, the Senate-house dedicated to St. Hadrian by Pope Honorius I., the church of S. Cyriacus, now called dei SS. Quirico e Giolitta; the church of St. Agatha, the Baths of Constantine, and the beautiful group of the Horse-tamers, from which the Quirinal hill borrowed its popular name of Monte Cavallo; and lastly, the four churches of S. Vitalis on the Vicus Longus (Via di S. Vitale), of S. Lorenzo in Panisperna, of Pudens, and of S. Euphemia on the Vicus Patricii (Via Urbana, Via del Bambino Gesù). All these churches are still extant except that of S. Euphemia, which was destroyed by Sixtus V. in 1587, while cutting open the new street between the Panisperna and S. Maria Maggiore. On the right two edifices only are mentioned, the Baths of Trajan and the Basilica of S. Pietro in Vincoli. Though in general it is true that the modern streets mentioned above, dei Banchi, del Pellegrino, delle Botteghe Oscure, etc., follow the lines of ancient thoroughfares, the statement must not be accepted too literally. There is usually a slight deviation to the right or to the left, in consequence of which the old pavements of basalt have come to light, as a rule, under the houses which flank the modern streets, rather than under the streets themselves.

The importance of the other section of this precious document, in which are transcribed some of the monumental inscriptions of the City, is almost as great as of that containing the *Itinerary*. I do not refer to inscriptions from the edifices which are still in existence, such as the arch of Claudius in the Via del Nazzareno, the obelisk of the Vatican, the column of Trajan, and the arch of Septimius Severus, but to those from buildings which have partly or wholly

FIG. 26. — The Ponte Salario, over the Anio, two miles north of Rome; blown up to prevent the advance of Garibaldi, in 1867.

disappeared. Following the order of the manuscript we find the first monument to be the bridge by which the Via Salaria crossed the river Anio, broken down first by Totila in 544, again by the Neapolitan army in 1798, and for the third time by the Pope's own soldiers in 1867 (Fig. 26).

Next in order are inscriptions from the square base of the mausoleum of Hadrian, the epitaphs of the great emperors of the second century buried within. The epitaphs were destroyed in July, 1579, by Pope Gregory XIII., who made use of the marbles for the decoration of the Cappella Gregoriana in St. Peter's. The document mentions furthermore the triumphal arch of Arcadius, Honorius, and Theodosius, which stood by the church of S. Orso at the entrance of the bridge of Nero (Pons Neronianus or Vaticanus); that of Gratian, Valentinian, and Theodosius, which stood by the church of S. Celso in Banchi, destroyed toward the end of the fifteenth century; and lastly an arch built by Titus at the curved end of the Circus Maximus, the fate of which is not known.

We find a reference also to a Nymphaeum, which was rebuilt in the fifth century by Flavius Philippus, prefect of the City, at the corner of the Via della Navicella (Vicus Capitis Africae) and Via dei SS. Quattro (Tabernola); we possess a drawing of it, made about 1500 by Peruzzi.[1] The monumental in-

[1] *C. I. L.* VI. 1728 a.

scriptions of the market (*macellum*) of Livia were still in place; they were afterwards made use of in the restoration of various churches, including that of S. Maria in Trastevere, two miles distant,[1] from the pavement of which they came to light again in 1868. The Baths of the Julii Akarii, which, according to another document of the Einsiedlen manuscript, stood near the island of S. Bartolomeo, are otherwise unknown. The Septizonium at the south corner of the Palatine hill seems already to have fallen into a ruinous condition. The inscription on the frieze of the lower colonnade numbered originally 280 letters, of which 118 could be copied by the Einsiedlen scribe, on the extreme left of the building toward the Circus Maximus, and 45 letters by the anonymous Barberinianus (*Cod.* XXX. 25) on the extreme right toward the arch of Constantine. There was consequently a gap of 117 letters between the two ends of the ruins, which were respectively called Septem Solia Maior and Septem Solia Minor. As the total length of the building was not far from three hundred feet, two-fifths had seemingly collapsed before or about the time of Charlemagne.[2]

Another inscription of the collection refers in a rather confused way to the repairs made by Arcadius and Honorius to the theatre of Pompey, which had

[1] *C. I. L.* VI. 1178.
[2] *Ruins and Excavations*, p. 183.

been half-ruined by an earthquake.[1] The Forum of Trajan and the Baths of Diocletian still retained some of their monumental inscriptions in place. The pavement of the Forum Romanum, of the Sacra Via, of the Vicus Tuscus, and of the Argiletum was still clear from any accumulation of rubbish, as shown by the fact that the compiler of the collection could copy the inscription of the Caballus Constantini, and others almost level with the pavement itself. He saw also several monuments on the Capitoline hill, and considerable remains of the embankment walls of the Tiber.[2] It appears, finally, that many tombs along the lonesome roads of the Campagna still retained their epitaphs and marble decorations, and that, here and there, the eye fell on an edict issued, centuries before, by some prefect of the City, such as the regulations against the frauds of the millers of the Janiculum, and of the customs officers stationed at the gates and posterns of the walls of Arcadius and Honorius.[3]

[1] *C. I. L.* VI. 1191.
[2] *Ibid.*, 472, 562, 773, 916, 1014, 1472, 1708.
[3] *Ibid.*, 1711, 1016, c.

CHAPTER XIV

THE USURPERS OF THE HOLY SEE, AND THE SACK OF 1084

THE two centuries between the pontificate of John VIII. (872–882) and that of Gregory VII. (1073–1085) witnessed the deepest degradation in the history of mediaeval Rome. As we follow the chain of events, roughly described in contemporary chronicles, we are often reminded of the time of the "thirty tyrants" in the third century of the Empire, the comparison being always in favour of these last.

We read of pontificates lasting only weeks or even days, as that of Boniface VI., which extended over fifteen days; of Theodore II., who was Pope for twenty days, and of Benedict V., who filled the chair of St. Peter for sixty-three days. There were forty-nine popes in two hundred years, and the succession was determined, not by established usage, but by the prevalence for the moment of one or another faction. Popes were elected in direct opposition to the statutes of canon law, as Marinus I. (882–884), Formosus (891–896), and John X. (914–928); elections were secured by an open purchase of votes, as that of Benedict

VIII.;[1] there was a double and even a triple election, — that of Sergius III. and John IX. in 898, and that of Benedict IX., Sylvester III., and Gregory VI. in 1045.

The supreme pontiff might be thrown into prison by his own attendants, as was Leo V., in 903, after reigning only 40 days; usurpers might in turn be expelled and shut up in a monastery, as Christopher was in 904; a pope might be strangled with a rope, or suffocated with pillows, or stabbed to the heart, as Stephen VI., Leo V., Christopher I., John X., John XII., Benedict VI.;[2] or chased from the chair of St. Peter, as Romanus was. The grave of a pope might be violated for the sake of the richly embroidered vestments in which the body had been buried, as was the tomb of Hadrian III., at Nonantola, in 885;[3] in one case the body itself was exhumed from before the high altar, slashed in the face and hands, mutilated, dragged on the floor of St. Peter's, and thrown into the river, — such a lot befell the corpse of Formosus in 896.[4]

Sepulchral inscriptions of popes in this period are still

[1] 1021–1024. The sum spent on this occasion is variously stated at 1000 to 2000 pounds of Papienses, or gold denarii coined at Pavia. See *Lib. Pont.* Vol. II. pp. 270, 275.

[2] De Rossi, *Inscr. Christ.* Vol. II. p. 215; Auxilius, *Defens. Formos.* ch. 10; *Lib. Pont.* Vol. II. p. 235, n. 1, p. 248, n. 18; Lintprand, *Autapod.* III. 43; Martinus Polonus in *Lib. Pont.* Vol. II. p. 240.

[3] *Lib. Pont.* Vol. II. p. 225, n. 3.

[4] "Ann. Alamann." in *Mon. Germ. Scr.* Vol. I. p. 53; Dümmler, *Auxilius und Vulgarius*, p. 95.

extant in which their predecessors are called "wolves"[1] and "unclean."[2] The sacred office was at the mercy of an unspeakable Theodora vestararia and a Marotia senatrix.[3] Patricians, like George Aventinensis and Gregory the Nomenclator,[4] were blinded, mutilated, and dragged from church to church. Matrons were punished by being stripped of their garments in the face of the populace and scourged till the blood ran, like Maria Superista.[5] There were fights in the streets, attacks on the castle of St. Angelo, appeals — often successful — to foreign invaders, famine, pestilence, fires, robberies, murders. The extent to which the moral sense of men was blunted may be inferred from the fact that the paternity of John XI. (931–936) is registered in the *Liber Pontificalis* in words that are unquotable. But it is only fair to remember that this shocking state of affairs did not prevail in Rome alone. The whole of Europe in those dark days was corrupt; yet, even in this period, we now and then find a pope of noble character, whose virtue, wisdom, and sanctity are in striking contrast with the tendencies of the age.

To what vicissitudes the remains of ancient Rome were subject in the tenth century it is easier to imagine than

---

[1] De Rossi, *Inscr. Christ.* Vol. II. p. 212.

[2] *Ibid.* p. 215, and *Lib. Pont.* Vol. II. p. 258, n. 4.

[3] *Chronicon of Benedict of Soracte*, ad a. 928.

[4] *Mon. Germ. Scr. Lang.* p. 483; *Ann. Fuld.* ad a. 882; Auxilius, *Defens. Formos.* ch. 4.

[5] *Mon. Germ. Scr. Lang.* p. 483.

to set forth in detail. Amidst general disorder and the strifes of contending factions, they became the prey of any one who had the power to seize them and use them for his own purposes. Some great buildings were transformed into strongholds; others were levelled to the ground to prevent their occupation by the opposite faction. A few were occupied by the lowest orders of tradespeople; thus the Forum Transitorium was taken possession of by the butchers, the Basilica Julia by the rope-makers, the Crypta Balbi by the candle-makers, and the Circus Flaminius by the lime-burners.

There was a decline in the number of pilgrims visiting the Holy City. Lack of knowledge — in regard to reading and writing — had extended so far that, after the double election of Sylvester and Gregory, in 1045, as both these popes were illiterate, a third pontiff was named who could help them celebrate the holy offices.[1]

The falling off in the number of pilgrims was manifest in the shrinkage of the "Pilgrim's Pence," the principal item in the revenue of the Holy See. This was due to the insecurity of travel not only in the Campagna, but also in the rest of Italy and in the Alpine passes. There were regular bands of highwaymen, organized to waylay the pilgrims and rob them of the pence that they were expecting to offer to the "great beggar," as Rome was called. Especially for pilgrims from the northern side

[1] See *Mon. Germ. Scr. Lang.* Vol. VI. p. 358 ad a. 1044.

of the Alps the journey to the "seat of the Apostles" involved risks and sufferings which now seem incredible. An inscription formerly in the parish church of Bourg-St.-Pierre, in the Val d'Entremont, recorded the murders committed by a band of Saracens in the St. Bernard Pass. These were the Moors of Frassineto, who for more than half a century, from 906 to 973, commanded the passes of the western Alps, exacting heavy ransoms from travellers, especially pilgrims. In 940 they crossed the St. Bernard and fell on the rich monastery of St. Maurice in the Rhone Valley. In 973, a distinguished pilgrim, Maiolus, abbot of Cluny, was taken at the bridge of Orsières, and compelled to pay a large sum in gold to save his life.

The outlaws of the Campagna vied in rapacity and cruelty with the Moors of Frassineto; and, although the popes of a later age succeeded in extirpating the evil, as regards the existence of regularly organized bands, yet the lonely roads converging to Rome have not until recently been quite secure. There exists still (at least, I saw it a few years ago) a modest wooden cross on the left bank of the ancient Via Clodia, opposite the so-called Sepoltura di Nerone, which marks the spot where a young female pilgrim was atrociously murdered in 1827.[1]

Toward the beginning of this troubled period the

[1] Shown in Fig. 17, p. 93.

loss of revenue from the contributions of pilgrims was temporarily offset by an increase from an unexpected source. In the pontificate of Stephen VI. (896–897), the venerable basilica of St. John Lateran fell in. Negligently built, with spoils from earlier edifices, as were the other churches of the time of Constantine, it had long since begun to show signs of decay. The walls of the nave rested on columns of various kinds of marble, differing in height and strength. These, yielding under the pressure of the roof, bulged outward so far that the ends of the beams of the roof-trusses came out of their sockets, and the building collapsed. In the basilica were untold treasures accumulated in the course of centuries; as Gaius Marius stole from the smouldering ruins of the temple of Jupiter on the Capitol (83 B.C.) several thousand pounds of gold, and Julius Caesar gathered large sums of money from the demolition of the temple of Pietas, near the Forum Holitorium, so the "usurpers of the Apostolic See bore from the basilica all its treasures, all its furniture of gold and silver, and all the utensils."

The chastisement that followed those evil days was sweeping, and introduced a new era, at least so far as the history of the papacy is concerned; and the fortunes of the papacy were always closely connected with the fate of the City. Robert Guiscard, Duke of Apulia, arrived in sight of the walls of Rome, May 24, 1084, and established his camp among the ruins of the aqueducts, probably on the same spot — by the Torre del Fiscale, fourth mile-stone of the Via Latina — where the Goths had encamped 547 years before. The Romans displayed more courage than might have been expected. Abandoned by the Emperor Henry IV., whom they had welcomed as a liberator only a few days previously, knowing what they had to expect at the hands of the Normans and Saracens, whom Gregory VII., Pope Hildebrand, had summoned to his rescue, they pluckily entered on the unequal fight. There were traitors among them, however, chief of whom was the consul Cencio Frangipane. At daybreak of May 28 the Normans and their infidel allies effected a double entrance by the Porta Flaminia (now Porta del Popolo) and the Porta Tiburtina (now Porta di S. Lorenzo); fighting their way through the eastern quarter of the city, they succeeded in releasing the Pope from the Castle of St. Angelo, and conducted him amid fire and carnage to the Lateran. The whole of the Campus Martius and of the Caelian hill was devastated by the flames, and the unhappy City became the scene of horrors, in comparison with which the sack of the Vandals seems merciful. On the third day the citizens tried to rise once more against their foes, but the attempt was stifled in blood and fire.

The scene is well pictured by Gregorovius. "When both flames and the tumult of battle had subsided," says the learned author of *Rome in the Middle Ages*,[1] "Rome lay a heap of smoking ashes before Gregory's eyes; burnt churches, streets in ruins, the dead bodies of Romans, formed a thousand accusers against him. The Pope must have averted his eyes as the Romans, bound with cords, were led in troops into their camp by Saracens. Noble women, men calling themselves senators, children, and youths were openly sold like cattle into slavery; others, and among them the imperial prefect, were carried as prisoners of state to Calabria. Goths and Vandals, nevertheless, had been more fortunate than were the Normans, since Goths and Vandals had found Rome filled with inexhaustible wealth, while the plunder of the Moslems in the service of the duke could no longer have been comparable to that which their predecessors had ravished from St. Peter's 230 years before. The city was now terribly impoverished, and even the churches were devoid of ornament. Mutilated statues stood in the ruinous streets or lay in the dust amid the relics of baths and temples. Hideous images of saints remained here and there in the basilicas, which were already falling into decay, and attracted the spoiler by the gold which was possibly still affixed to them by votaries. The brutal fury of the victors satisfied itself for some days in robbery and murder, until the Romans, a sword and a cord round their necks, threw themselves at the feet of the duke. The grim conqueror

[1] Mrs. Hamilton's translation, Vol. IV. p. 246.

felt compassion, but he could not make good their losses."

Even after the lapse of so many centuries, we can still find in Rome traces of this Norman-Saracenic invasion. The Caelian quarter as a whole has never recovered from the state of desolation to which it was reduced in 1084 (Fig. 27). The few roads which traverse this silent region are practically the same as those through which Gregory VII. had been hurried from the castle of S. Angelo to the Lateran; only their present level is higher, the layer of débris from the burnt edifices having considerably raised the level of the whole district. We have evidence of this in the two churches of S. Clemente, one above the other. The lower church shows the level of the city before, and the upper that after, the fire. The reconstruction of S. Clemente was undertaken, after the withdrawal of Robert Guiscard, by Cardinal Anastasius, who died in 1126 or 1128, leaving the completion of the work to Cardinal Pietro Pisano. This information has lately been obtained from the epitaph of Cardinal Pisano, which was accidentally discovered in the foundations of a new house in Via Arenula. The marble slab on which this inscription was cut appears to have been divided up into small squares, at an unknown date, to pave a room in a house two miles distant from S. Clemente. There is a difference in level of thirteen feet and seven inches between the earlier and the later church.

FIG. 27. — View of the Caelian hill, looking southeast.

The fate of another ecclesiastical building on the Caelian, the church of the SS. Quattro Coronati, destroyed by the same fire, is somewhat different. This church was rebuilt by Paschal II. in 1111 on the same level, for the reason that the débris of the fire had evidently rolled down the slopes of the knoll on which the building stood, but it occupies only a small portion of the original area. We learn from the inscription of Paschal II., still extant, that he made excavations under the marble floor in search of some holy relics: *iussit cavare sub altare quod prius combustum et confractum fuerat et invenit duas concas unam porphireticam et aliam ex proconesso in quibus erant recondita sacra corpora.* The work was not completed till January 7, 1116. To the same Pope is due also the reconstruction of the churches of S. Adriano in the Forum Romanum (1110), of S. Maria in Monticelli, of S. Pantaleo ai Monti (1113), of S. Salvatore in Primicerio (1113), and of a chapel near the Porta Flaminia, erected to scare away the ghost of Nero, by which it was believed that belated travellers were pursued on entering the city.

Much has been written in regard to the extent of the damage done to the pagan monuments by the pillage and fire of 1084. It must have been great, especially in the region of the Caelian, of the Oppian, and of the valley which runs between these hills in the direction of the Lateran. The old Porta Asinaria was named, after the catastrophe, the Porta Perusta, or the "burnt gate."

In fact, the final decay of the City,—the abandonment of the old level of streets and squares (Fig. 28), the disappearance of the remains of private houses, and even of some public edifices,—dates from this fearful conflagration. The hills, long since stricken by water famine, now ceased altogether to be inhabited, and the scanty population pressed more and more toward the Campus Martius, where the digging of wells was easier on account of the alluvial soil which forms the valley of the Tiber. The larger monuments, such as temples, theatres, and baths, were not much damaged by the fire. The columns of Trajan and of Marcus Aurelius did not suffer at all, being in the middle of open squares. The collection of works of art in bronze at the Lateran, and that of marble statues on the Quirinal, also went safely through the ordeal. Hildebert, Archbishop of Tours, who visited Rome in 1106 or 1107, speaks of great remains which struck him with admiration, and also of the beautiful statues in which the City still abounded.

We know one of the reasons, at least, why the two massive columns of Trajan and of Marcus Aurelius were spared in these centuries of wholesale destruction. They brought a respectable income to their respective owners, namely, to the public treasury for the first, and to the monks of SS. Dionysius and Sylvester for the second. An inscription in the vestibule of the present church of S. Silvestro in Capite, dated 1119, states that both the column of Marcus Aurelius and the little church

FIG. 28. — View of the Forum in 1821, partly excavated, showing the difference between the ancient and the modern level.

of St. Nicholas which stood at the foot of it were leased to the highest bidder, probably from year to year, on account of the fees which could be collected from the tourist or pilgrim that wished to behold the wonders of Rome from a lofty point of observation.

The obelisks were less fortunate than the commemorative columns just referred to, and the overthrowing of the obelisk set up by Augustus as a sun-dial in the Campus Martius is commonly attributed to the Normans. This shaft was undoubtedly erect on its pedestal in the time of Charlemagne, when the Einsiedlen *Itinerary* was compiled; but we are not sure whether, after all, the Normans are to be held responsible for its destruction. Were we in possession of precise records of the discovery of the different obelisks, indicating the way in which they lay on their bed of rubbish, the depth at which the various fragments were found, the injuries that they had received before, during, or after the fall, and the nature of the fractures, we should probably be able to tell by what agency the giants were laid low. But it is certain that the responsibility of the throwing down of the monoliths cannot be fixed upon the early barbarian invaders, because we know that some of the principal obelisks were still standing in the sixth and seventh centuries. Nor can earthquakes be considered an adequate cause; why should the Vatican obelisk have been the only one to withstand the shocks? Further, it has been proved that the columns of the porticoes of public and private buildings destroyed by the earthquake of 422 all fell in the same direction, toward the northeast, that is, toward the point of the compass from which the shock came. The obelisks, on the contrary, appear to have fallen toward every point on the horizon.

The last statement is corroborated by the evidence of the first man who investigated the subject, Michele Mercati.[1] He states that the obelisks discovered by his contemporary, Sixtus V., — the two from the Circus Maximus, now in the Piazza del Laterano and the Piazza del Popolo, and the one from the mausoleum of Augustus, now in the Piazza dell' Esquilino — had not been overthrown by accidental causes. They all retained evidence of the efforts made by man to bring them down, by drilling holes to insert levers, or by building fires about the pedestal. He says that every obelisk which he saw come out of the ground was broken into three pieces, the upper and middle pieces being intact, while the lower portion, which rested on the base, showed the edges rounded off by the violence of the flames. Such operations require more time and patience than would have been devoted to such a purpose by the barbarians.

I have three documents to present in relation to this interesting subject of the fate of the obelisks. One is an unpublished sketch by Carlo Fontana, showing the

[1] See p. 152 of his book *Degli obelischi di Roma*, MDLXXXIX.

way the obelisk of the gardens of Sallust lay at the moment of its discovery. Another is a sketch by Angelo Maria Bandini, showing the injuries which the lower portion of the obelisk of the Campus Martius had suffered before or at the time of its fall; and lastly, the record of my own experience in unearthing the obelisk of the temple of Isis, near the apse of the church of La Minerva.

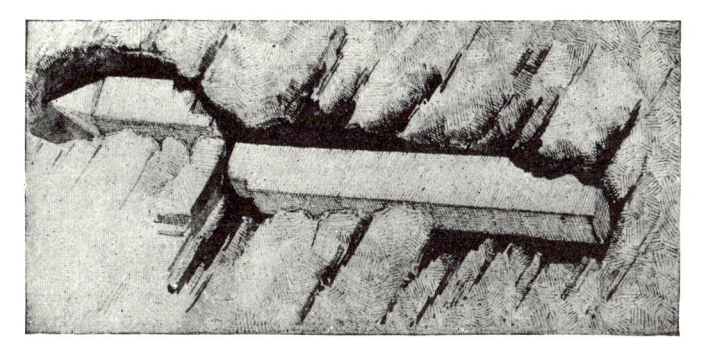

FIG. 29. — The obelisk of the gardens of Sallust, as it lay after it had fallen.

The sketch of Carlo Fontana, here reproduced (Fig. 29), is dated March 21, 1706, and is preserved in the private library of Queen Victoria at Windsor.[1] It shows the way in which one of the obelisks decorating the Egyptian casino of the gardens of Sallust had fallen, having been broken into two pieces, one double the length of the other. This division of parts is especially interesting in the light of Mercati's statement that in

[1] Volume G 1, sheet 249.

their fall the obelisks would generally break into three pieces of about equal length.

The drawing given by Bandini[1] to illustrate the condition of the obelisk in the Campus Martius is even more significant. I have reproduced it on a scale a little less than one third the size of the original (Fig. 30).

This drawing shows how the lower portion of the monolith had been eaten away and rounded off by fire; we can see also the holes drilled in the upper part for the insertion of levers and iron clamps, by those who were endeavouring to hasten the fall of the shaft. But the chief importance

[1] *De Obelisco Cæsaris Augusti, e Campi Martii ruderibus nuper eruto.* Romae, MDCCL.

FIG. 30.—The obelisk of the Campus Martius.

lies in the fact that from the evidence thus afforded we are able to determine the approximate date of the fall itself. The reader will observe that though the shaft is greatly injured and in part calcined, the pedestal is in a remarkable state of preservation. The meaning of this is clear — the shaft was protruding above ground and exposed to injury, while the base was embedded in and protected by the soil and débris which had accumulated around it. In other words, when the obelisk of Augustus fell, the level of the Campus Martius had risen some ten or eleven feet; it was about halfway between the classical and the modern level of the City. We may, therefore, assign the fall of the monolith to the tenth or the eleventh century.

In a line with this conclusion was the condition of the obelisk of Rameses the Great, which was brought to light June 14, 1883, among the ruins of the temple of Isis.[1] When this graceful monument was laid on its side, the pavement of the temple in which it was standing had already been covered with a thick layer of rubbish.

[1] *Bull. Com.*, 1883, p. 33 sq.

CHAPTER XV

ROME AT THE END OF THE TWELFTH CENTURY — THE ITINERARY OF BENEDICT

THE state of Rome before and after the Norman invasion could in no way be more clearly indicated than by comparing the Einsiedlen *Itinerary*, of the ninth century, with the *Itinerary* of Benedict, of the twelfth. This last document, better known under the name of *Ordo Romanus*, forms a part of the *Liber politicus* written by Benedict, who was canon of St. Peter's under the pontificate of Innocent II. (1130–1143). It was dedicated to Guy of Castello, cardinal of St. Mark. Benedict himself became Pope in 1143, under the name of Caelestinus II. His *Ordo*, edited by Mabillon, Urlichs, Jordan, and myself,[1] describes seven routes by which the popes used to cross the city at the head of public processions on certain days of the year. They are as follows: —

---

[1] Mabillon, *Museum Italicum*, Vol. II. p. 143, nn. 50, 51; Urlichs, *Codex topographicus urbis Romae*, p. 79 sq.; Jordan, *Topographie der Stadt Rom in Altertum*, Vol. II. p. 664 sq.; Lanciani, *L'Itinerario di Einsiedlen*, p. 87 sq.

THE ITINERARY OF BENEDICT

ROUTE

I. From the church of the Resurrection (now S. Anastasia) to St. Peter's.

II. From the church of St. Hadrian to S. Maria Maggiore.

III. From the church of S. Maria Maggiore to the Lateran.

IV. From the Lateran to the Vatican, and

V. Back from the Vatican to the Lateran by a different route.

VI. From the Coliseum to St. Peter's.

VII. From the church of S. Maria Nuova (now S. Francesca Romana) to S. Maria Maggiore.

These seven routes correspond in part with those followed by the Einsiedlen *Itinerary*, and are specially important for our study; a greater number of landmarks are mentioned than in the Einsiedlen document, and many changes are clearly seen to have taken place in the thoroughfares of the City since the ninth century. We may also observe that, while the Einsiedlen *Itinerary* is based on a map of the City of the fourth or fifth century, made at a time when the edifices still bore their correct and classic names, the *Itinerary* of Benedict has a distinctly mediaeval character, and shows traces of the influence of that widely used mediaeval guide-book, "The Marvels of Rome" (*Mirabilia Urbis Romae*).[1] In fact, Benedict the Canon apparently had at hand no better source of information for topography, when describing the pontifical pageants through the City, than this vade mecum of ignorant pilgrims, which

[1] There is an English translation by F. M. Nichols, London. 1889.

had gradually made its way among the official documents of the Roman curia, as did the *Politicus* of Benedict and the *liber Censuum* of Cencius Camerarius.

It will be instructive to compare the Tenth Route of the Einsiedlen *Itinerary* with the First of the *Itinerary* of Benedict; both conduct the reader over the same ground, between the Circus Maximus and the Crypta Balbi. The first mentions the following objects of interest: —

Ecclesia Graecorum, now the church of S. Maria in Cosmedin.
Scola Graecorum, now Piazza della Bocca della Verità.
Templum Jovis, temple of Jupiter Optimus Maximus, on the Capitoline hill.
Elephantus, i.e. Elephantus Herbarius, on the Via della Bocca della Verità.
Porticus, colonnade on the west side of the Via della Bocca della Verità.
Theatrum, theatre of Marcellus.
Sanctus Angelus, the colonnade of Octavia.
Porticus, the colonnade of Philippus.
Theatrum Pompeii, the theatre of Pompey.

These names, we readily see, all belong to the classical or Byzantine periods. But the names of the *Ordo* are of an altogether different class, and their relation to the names given in the *Mirabilia* is at once obvious. We start from the church of the Anastasis, which has already been transformed into Sancta Anastasia, and follow Benedict over the same route. The Porticus usque ad Elephantum has become the *Porticus Galla-*

torum, now represented by the church and hospital of S. Galla Patricia; the temples of Pietas and Hope in the Forum Holitorium have the name of *Cicero* and the *Sibyl;* the theatre of Marcellus is a *Basilica Jovis;* the Porticus Minucia is now the *Porticus Crinorum*, and the Crypta Balbi is a *Templum Craticulae.*

A similar shifting from ancient to mediaeval names is to be found in every route of the *Ordo;* nevertheless this will always remain a document of the first rank for our knowledge of monumental Rome in the twelfth century. To indicate its value we may take up the part dealing with the Burgus, or Vatican district, which is not covered by the Einsiedlen *Itinerary;* the topographical outline, accurate as well as clear, is as follows: —

1. *Pons, templum, castellum Adriani*, now the bridge and castle of S. Angelo.
2. *Porta collina*, the gate of St. Peter, in front of the castle, destroyed by Alexander VI.
3. *Obeliscus Neronis*, the familiar Terebinth of the *Mirabilia*, one of the great mausolea on the border of the Via Triumphalis.

    Peter Mallius describes this mausoleum as resembling in shape and in height the mole of Hadrian. It was demolished to take advantage of its beautiful marbles for the building of the steps and of the court of St. Peter's. The name Terebinthus seems to be a corruption of *tiburtinum*, which in the language of those days meant an edifice built of stone or marble. Antonio Filarete has represented the monument, in one of the panels of the bronze gates, as actually having the shape of a tree![1]

[1] The name for turpentine-tree in Italian is *terebinto.*

4. *Memoria seu sepulcrum Romuli*, Tomb of Romulus.

This "Tomb of Romulus" was a mausoleum of pyramidal shape, so called to form a pair with the so-called Meta Remi, which we know as the pyramid of Cestius, by the Porta di S. Paolo. It was also popularly called Meta di Borgo, and is represented in Antonio Filarete's bronze panel, as well as in Raphael's fresco of the Vision of Constantine. It stood on the left of the Via Triumphalis, between the church of S. Maria Transpontina and the palazzo Giraud-Torlonia in the Piazza Scossa-Cavalli. Alexander VI. levelled it to the ground to make room for his Via Alexandrina.

5. *Porticus, Porticus Maior, Via Sacra.*

This was a covered way, by means of which the pilgrims could cross the Borgo under shelter. It started at the Ponte S. Angelo, and followed the line of the present Borgo Vecchio to the foot of the steps of St. Peter's.

6. *S. Laurentius in Porticu Maiore.*

The covered way just mentioned was lined with churches and shrines, such as S. Maria Transpontina de Capite Porticus, demolished July 13, 1564; S. Salvator de Porticu, or de Bordonia, now represented by S. Giacomo Scossa-Cavalli; and the S. Laurentius of the *Ordo*, rebuilt in its present shape by the Cesi d' Acquasparta in 1659.

7. *S. Maria in Virgari.*

This was a church at the end of the covered way, toward St. Peter's, so called from the corporation of makers and sellers of pilgrims' staffs, to which it belonged. Pius IV. demolished it in 1568 to widen the area mentioned under the next head.

8. *Cortina Beati Petri.*

This was a small square at the foot of the steps of St. Peter's, ornamented with three fountains, one of which was of porphyry; the other two were of white marble.

Interesting as it would be to follow the worthy canon through the other parts of the City, the limits of our task forbid. Mediaeval Rome has now almost reached the limit of its greater changes. The level of the ancient City in most places lies ten or twelve feet below the surface. A large portion of the site of the once proud metropolis is wholly deserted; the great monuments, moss-grown and crumbling except where the solidity of

FIG. 31. — A typical Roman house of the twelfth century, built with odd fragments.

construction was such as to defy Nature herself, are in part turned to account as habitations, in part exploited for such building materials as are of use to the scanty population of degenerate days (Fig. 31), in part left undisturbed in the midst of the wilderness.

CHAPTER XVI

MARBLE-CUTTERS AND LIME-BURNERS OF MEDIAEVAL AND RENAISSANCE ROME

In the exploiting of the Roman monuments for valuable materials in mediaeval and early modern times, two classes of workmen in particular wrought the most serious damage. These were the Marmorarii, or marble-cutters, and the Calcararii, or lime-burners.

The Roman marble-cutters, architects, sculptors, and mosaic-makers, whose work was in a sense a precursor of the Renaissance, whose artistic creations still command our admiration, are generally called the "School of Cosmatis." The Cosmatis, however, are only a branch of this great succession of workmen which was founded, about 1150, by the Sons of Paul, *filii Pauli*. Lawrence, son of Cosmas, the head of the Cosmati branch, flourished toward the end of the twelfth century, and was followed by five generations of artists of the same name. The Vassalecti form the third branch, which also includes three or four generations, from 1153 to 1275; the last branch is that of Ranuccio Romano, with his sons Peter and Nicholas, his nephew John Guittone, and his grandson John, who flourished from 1143 to 1209.

It is not necessary to repeat here what Promis, Reumont, De Rossi, Frothingham, Richter, Boni, Mazzanti, and others have written on the origin and progress of this great school of marble-cutters. For our purposes it is sufficient to observe that for the space of three centuries the guild lived and prospered and accomplished its work at the expense of the ruins of ancient Rome. The marble-workers made excavations and destroyed old monuments with two ends in view, to find models and to secure materials for their work. They were especially fond of epitaphs — whether pagan or Christian it mattered not — because the thin slabs of marble on which the epitaphs were inscribed could easily be adapted to their purpose, being almost ready for use in borders and panels of mosaic, ambones, and decorative patterns. This is the reason why the floors of our mediaeval churches are so rich in epigraphic documents; about two hundred inscriptions were used in making the pavement of SS. Quattro Coronati after the destruction of the church by the Normans, and nearly a thousand were similarly turned to use in the floor of St. Paul's without the Walls.

The marble-workers also inaugurated an interprovincial and even international traffic in Roman marbles, which flourished for two and a half centuries, sustained by the spirit of emulation in building which had seized the cities of Italy. Each town felt impelled to raise a church, "grand, beautiful, magnificent, whose just proportions in height, breadth, and length should so harmonise with the details of the decoration as to make it decorous and solemn, and worthy of the worship of Christ in hymns and canticles," like the duomo of Siena; and campaniles which should reach "even to the stars," like that of Spoleto.

The first influential voice heard in remonstrance against these practices of the marble-cutters, and the utter abandonment of the Roman monuments, is that of Petrarch. His pungent remarks were addressed especially to the nobles, whom he describes as following in the path of destruction, treading in the footsteps of the Goths and the Vandals. However, if the patricians were to blame, the middle and lower classes closely followed their example. Temples, baths, theatres, and palaces were demolished piecemeal; their marble ornaments were broken to pieces and thrown into the lime-kilns, and even their walls overthrown and their foundations broken up for the sake of the stones or of the bricks with which they were faced. After a time the produce of this industry grew in excess of the demand, and more spoils were accumulated than could be disposed of in the local market.

Some of the facts connected with this new phase in the history of the destruction of Rome are known to students; but they have yet to be properly grouped and compared. I shall here offer only a few observations, with the hope that they may induce others to investigate the subject more thoroughly. The archives of our great church buildings have yet to be explored; the success achieved by Luigi Fumi in examining the documents connected with the building of the duomo at Orvieto leads us to hope that other records may be found, on both sides of the Alps, by means of which this branch of trade of mediaeval Rome may be illustrated.

The earliest instance of the removal of marbles from the Eternal City to distant lands dates from the time of King Theoderic. In a letter addressed to Festus the Patrician, Cassiodorius, the king's secretary, orders that the columns of the Domus Pinciana — an imperial possession near the gate of the same name — should be sent to Ravenna.

The portion of the cathedral of Aix-la-Chapelle erected by Charlemagne in 796–804, and consecrated by Leo III., is an octagon copied from S. Vitale at Ravenna, designed and built by Roman marmorarii. The lofty openings of the upper story are decorated with a double row of columns of unequal length, of rare marbles and breccias, brought from Rome, Trèves, and Ravenna.[1] In fact, the desire to follow Roman traditions was so great that the fountain in front of the cathedral was actually decorated with a brazen wolf, like the one which then stood in front of the Lateran, and with a pine cone, like the one which stood on the fountain of Symmachus, in the atrium of St. Peter's.

[1] The most valuable were stolen by the French invaders in 1794, but restored at the peace of 1815.

The cathedral of Pisa, begun in 1063, and consecrated in 1118 by Pope Gelasius II., is mostly built of marbles taken from Rome and Ostia. The workshop in which the classic remains were transformed into new shapes by Busketus and Ronald, the architects of the duomo, has lately been found on the banks of the Arno. Some of the marbles actually bear the mark of their origin; one near the southwest corner of the transept is inscribed GENIO · COLONIAE · OSTIENSIS, "To the Genius of Ostia." They also imported sarcophagi, as that discovered in 1742 at the foot of the high altar, and now preserved in the Camposanto, inscribed with the name of Marcus Annius Proculus, a magistrate and leading citizen of Ostia.

The inexhaustible stores of Rome were resorted to for the construction of the cathedrals of Lucca (1060–1070) and of Monte Cassino (1066); of those of S. Mattéo at Salerno (1084; Fig. 32), and of S. Andrea at Amalfi (eleventh century); of the baptistery of S. Giovanni in Florence (begun in 1100); of the monastery of Nostra Signora di Tergu, on the north coast of Sardinia, between Sorso and Castel Sardo, of the church of S. Francesco at Città Vecchia, of the cathedral of Orvieto (1321–1360), and even of some parts of Westminster Abbey. To prove this statement in the case of some of the buildings we need no literary evidence; the shape and quality of the marbles, and the inscriptions engraved upon them, give unmistakable testimony regarding their origin. Yet for Monte Cassino we do have the authority of Alphanus and of Leo of Ostia, who expressly state that Desiderius

FIG. 32. — The pulpit in the cathedral of S. Mattéo at Salerno, built with marbles from Rome.

purchased in Rome "columns, bases, and capitals, and marbles of various colours." These spoils were put on board light coasting ships (*tartane*) like those that still sail up the Tiber to the wharf of Ripa Grande, and landed at the mouth of the Garigliano. From the mouth of the Garigliano to Monte Cassino the work of transportation was accomplished with teams of buffaloes. One consequence of the sack of 1084 was the carrying off of columns and marbles of various kinds by the retiring army for the adornment of the cathedral at Salerno.

We are indebted to Luigi Fumi for detailed information concerning the use of materials from Rome in the building of the cathedral at Orvieto.[1] The first barge-loads were shipped up the Tiber, from the quay of the Ripetta to Orte, in June, 1316. For the space of nearly forty years the *maestri dell' Opera del' duomo*, or "superintendents of construction," sent their agents through the country around Rome in search of blocks of marble for their carvings. The ruins of Porto (the Portus Augusti, near the mouth of the Tiber) were attacked in May, 1321, with the consent of their owners; those of Ostia, then probably not subject to individual ownership, shared the same fate in the following year — the centre of devastation being the theatre, the shattered remains of which I brought to light in 1881.

In process of time the villa of Domitian at Castel Gandolfo, the mausoleum of Hadrian, the portico of Octavia, the temple of Isis and Serapis, and the ruins of Veii were in like manner put to ransom. The docu-

[1] Fumi, *Il duomo di Orvieto ed i suoi restauri*, Rome, 1881.

ments collected by Fumi give us many details of this remarkable trade in old marbles. Pandolfo and Giovanni Savelli, who had placed at the disposal of the builders of the cathedral the remains of the villa of Domitian, were remunerated with a gift of pepper, wax, and saffron. In 1354, while Andrea di Ugolino was superintending the work, a block of marble purchased for thirty-five florins was taken from the colonnade of Octavia, and cut into the beautiful round window which occupies the centre of the façade. Other blocks were brought from the same source in 1359, under the mastership of Andrea d' Orcagna. When search was made in private grounds a compensation was paid to the owner, as in the case of the colonnade of Octavia, and of the temple of Isis, which belonged respectively to Alessio Matrice and to Paolo di Converrone. If the blocks were considered *res nullius*, a fee was paid to the City for the license of exportation.

Giacomo Boni, in a paper read at a meeting of the British and American Society of Rome, March 28, 1893, makes an interesting statement regarding the use of Roman materials in Westminster Abbey. "Among the most important works of a Roman marble-cutter still preserved in Westminster Abbey," he says, "there is a small tomb bearing no inscription, but believed to be of the daughter of Henry III., who died in 1257. The name of PETRVS ROMANVS CIVIS is engraved in the basement of the shrine of Edward the Confessor. Peter, therefore, must have worked on it toward 1269, the year in which the relics of the Confessor were laid in the place of honour by Henry III. The tomb of this king, the second founder of Westminster Abbey, erected in 1281, has nothing English about it, save the grey Purbeck marble. The materials of which the Romanesque pavement in front of the high altar is composed were certainly imported from Rome by the Abbot Richard of Ware. After his election, which took place in 1258, the abbot paid a visit to the Eternal City, and brought back, as a souvenir of his pilgrimage, some slabs of porphyry and serpentine. Upon his grave may be read the following words: —

HIC PORTAT LAPIDES QVOS HVC PORTAVIT AB VRBE,

that is to say, he lies buried under the red and green porphyries (the essential element of a Romanesque pavement) which he brought himself from the banks of the Tiber to those of the Thames."

The attempt of Richard of Ware to transplant to England a style of work which could only find its proper means of support among the ruins of an ancient city, was not successful; but there is no doubt — although we yet lack material evidence — that the Romans found new outlets for their trade to compensate for the loss of the English market.

In presenting this aspect of the destruction of the Eternal City, I do not wish to cast more blame on the mediaeval marble-cutters than they actually deserve. Much may be said in extenuation of their treatment of ancient buildings; and many instances of more wanton destruction might be cited, from the time of Nero to our own age. While the army of Vespasian was besieging the Capitol, and trying to scale its walls from the roofs of the nearest houses, the partisans of Vitellius hurled bronze and marble statues on their assailants; and the garrison of Hadrian's mausoleum, as we have seen, defended themselves in a similar manner during the siege of the Goths. Self-defence may be urged as a legitimate excuse; but I have discovered in the State archives a petition addressed on August 20, 1822, to Pope Pius VII. by a building contractor, named Mattéo Lovatti, in which he states that, to provide materials for a house he was raising in the Piazza del Popolo, he would like to destroy certain ancient ruins opposite the church of S. Maria in Dominica. It is astonishing to think that such a request could have been addressed to a man like Pope Pius VII., and more so to know that the request was granted, on the favourable report of Visconti, Fea, Valadier, and Cardinal Pacca.

In 1870, a few months before Rome became the capital of Italy, Pope Pius IX. determined to raise a monumental column in memory of the Ecumenical Council. To save time and money, and the trouble of quarrying travertine from the territory of Tivoli, one of the most interesting and best preserved gates of the City, the

Porta Tiburtina of Honorius, was sacrificed. The stones of which it was built were sunk in the foundations of the column, opposite the church of S. Pietro in Montorio — all to no purpose, because the events of September 20 of that year made the raising of the monument out of the question.

We have already seen that Roman legislation at one time imposed capital punishment on those who destroyed old tombs for the sake of the marble of which they were built, and that Constans substituted a fine for the death penalty; and that these and similar provisions for a time checked the destruction of the tombs lying close to the highways, while those less exposed to view, or standing on private grounds, were ruthlessly sacrificed.[1] The destruction did not decrease in the Middle Ages, and waxed even greater in the Renaissance. Chrysoloras, the master of Poggio Bracciolini, says, referring to marbles taken from this source: "The statues lie broken in fragments, ready for the lime-kiln, or are made use of as building material. I have seen many used as mounting-steps, or as curbstones, or as mangers in stables."

Public officials not only tolerated this search for sculptured marbles and for limestone, but sometimes claimed a share in the profits. From a document of July 1, 1426, preserved in the Vatican archives,[2] we learn that

[1] See p. 92.   [2] *Diversorum*, Vol. IX. p. 245.

the papal authorities, while giving a free hand to a company of lime-burners to destroy the Basilica Julia on the Sacra Via for the sake of the blocks of travertine of which the pillars of the nave and aisles were built, reserved to themselves half the produce of the kilns; a present was afterward made of the income from this source to Cardinal Giacomo Isolani, who was then engaged in repairing his titular church of S. Eustachio. A fate similar to that of the Basilica Julia fell to the lot of the tomb of Alexander Severus at the Monte del Grano; thus perished also half of the Coliseum, the arch of Lentulus, the Circus Maximus, the square basement of the mausoleum of Caecilia Metella, and a hundred other monuments, the spoils of which served to build St. Peter's, St. Mark's, the Palazzo di Corneto, the Palazzo Farnese, the Cancelleria, the Villa Giulia. "In the early years of Paul III." (1534-1550), says De Marchi, "many torsoes and statues discovered in digging cellars, in planting gardens and vineyards, and in opening new streets, used to be thrown into the kilns, especially those sculptured in Greek marble, on account of the wonderful lime which they produced. Paul III. issued most cruel regulations to the effect that no one should dare thus to destroy ancient statuary under penalty of death. The result was a steady increase in the number and value of public and private archaeological collections in Rome."[1]

[1] See the article by Müntz in *Revue Archéologique* for May-June, 1884.

As a matter of fact, however, these "most cruel regulations" of Paul III. did not produce a lasting effect. We may suppose that the destruction of the masterpieces of Greco-Roman art may have diminished for the time being, but it was by no means suppressed. The spoliation of marble and stone edifices went on with increasing activity to the end of the sixteenth century. We must not forget that another edict of the same Pope, dated July 22, 1540, put at the mercy of the "deputies" of the Fabbrica di S. Pietro all the monuments of the Forum and of the Sacra Via; and they did not hesitate to profit by the pontifical grant to the fullest possible extent.

Pirro Ligorio, the architect, discussing the best way of obtaining a particularly fine plaster, suggests the use of powdered Parian marble, "obtained from the statues which are constantly being destroyed."[1] Flaminio Vacca, after describing a certain marble boat with figures on it, found in the Baths of Caracalla, remarks that "as it once floated on water, so now it has been made to steer its way through fire." He makes a similar observation with respect to a statue found by Orazio Muti, opposite the church of S. Vitale, "which had been sent to the kiln to have the moisture taken off its back."[2] Thousands of inscriptions have perished in the same way. Fra Giocondo da Verona, adducing testimony from his

[1] Ligorio, *Codex Bodleianus*, p. 17.
[2] Flaminio Vacca, *Memorie*, edited by Fea, n. 23, 116.

own experience, says that some Roman citizens boasted of having had the foundations of their houses and palaces constructed with ancient statues.

The headquarters of these destroyers of ancient Rome was at the "Botteghe Oscure," that is, in the wing of the Circus Flaminius facing the street of that name — the arcades were then in a good state of preservation, and high above ground; but, as a matter of fact, there was no great ruin of marble or stone that did not have its own kiln. So important was the exercise of this industry of lime-burning at the Circus Flaminius that the whole district received the name of Lime-pit (*calcarario, calcararia*). The extent of the area covered by this designation can be determined by the site of the churches of S. Nicolaus in Calcaria retro Cesarinos, now S. Nicola ai Cesarini, SS. Quaranta de Calcarario, now S. Francesco delle Stimmate, and S. Lucia de Calcarario, now S. Lucia dei Ginnasi; there was also a spring named *Il Calcarario*, in the Piazza dell' Olmo.

Other famous kilns were those of S. Adriano, for the burning of the marbles of the Imperial Forums; of the *Agosta*, fed with the spoils of the mausoleum of Augustus; and of *La Pigna*, supplied with materials from the Baths of Agrippa and the temple of Isis. Then there were temporary establishments opened near this or that edifice, which were abandoned as soon as the supply was exhausted. We must class among these the kilns by the Baths of Diocletian, mentioned by Flaminio Vacca; those of the villa of Livia at Prima Porta, mentioned by Pirro Ligorio; those of the necropolis between the Via Latina and the Via Appia, seen by Marini; those of the Regia, described by Panvinio, and those of the Basilica Julia, and of the temple of Venus and Rome, discovered by Nibby and by myself.[1]

Outside the City the burning of lime was practised for many years among the ruins of Ostia and Porto. The oldest record bearing upon the matter, that is known to me, is a document of Celestine III., dated March 30, 1191, where mention is made of a "*locus qui vocatur calcaria extra portam non longe ab Hostiensi civitate.*"[2] The exercise of this trade continued without interruption and with the tacit, if not open, approval of the papal authorities, down to the pontificate of Pius VII. Fea relates the following incident: "To the insatiable greed" of Giuseppe Vitelli, tenant of the farm at Ostia in the year 1816, "is due the disappearance of some miles of the paving of the ancient Ostian way, which was in a most excellent state of preservation, as well as the destruction of many large pieces of carved cornice from the temple of Vulcan, a masterpiece of the time of Hadrian. . . . He broke the latter into frag-

---

[1] Flaminio Vacca, *Memorie*, 104; Ligorio, *Codex Neapolitanus*, 29; Marini, *Inscriptiones alb.* X.; Pauvinio, see *C. I. L.* Vol. I. p. 415; *Bull. del Inst.*, 1871, p. 244.

[2] *Bullarium Vaticanum*, Vol. III. p. 75.

ments to make lime in a kiln close by; but I succeeded in stopping him before the fagots were set on fire." The fragments thus rescued from the flames are still shown on the spot (Fig. 33). Other pieces of this exquisite entablature had been destroyed in 1427, before the eyes of Poggio Bracciolini and Cosimo de' Medici. Similar kilns were discovered in 1796 by Robert Fagan, not far from the temple.

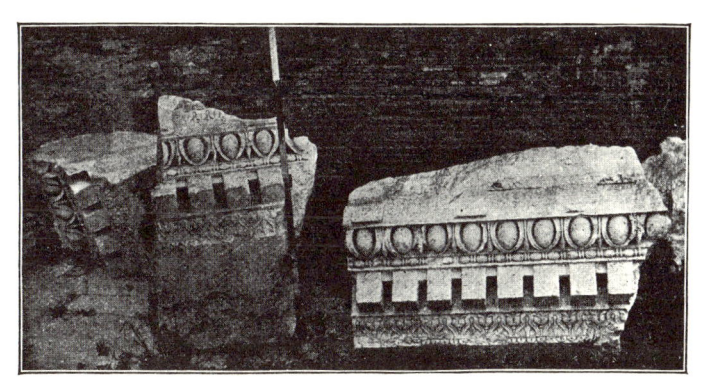

FIG. 33. — Fragments of cornice from the temple of Vulcan, at Ostia, rescued from a lime-kiln by Fea.

I have myself had no small experience in tracing the results of the operations of the lime-burners; in fact, none of the important excavations with which I have been connected, either in Rome or on neighbouring sites, has failed to bring to light remains of one or more lime-kilns. I mention two examples as specially worthy of note.

A lime-kiln was found in the palace of Tiberius on

the Palatine hill by Rosa, in 1869. It was filled to the brim with fine works of art, some calcined, some intact. Among the latter were the veiled bust of Claudius, now in the Museo delle Terme; a head of Nero; three caryatides, in nero antico; the exquisite little statuette of an ephebus in black basalt, published by Hauser in the *Mittheilungen* for 1895, p. 97–119, pl. 1; a head of Harpocrates, and other minor fragments.

In February, 1883, in the excavations on the south side of the Atrium of Vesta, a pile of marble was found about 14 feet long, 9 feet wide, and 7 feet high. It was wholly made up of statues of the *Vestales maximae*, some unbroken, others in fragments. The statues and fragments had been carefully packed together, leaving as few interstices as possible between them, and the spaces formed by the curves of the bodies were filled in with chips. There were eight nearly perfect statues, and we were agreeably surprised to find among the broken ones the lower part of the lovely seated Vesta with the footstool, which alas! is now hardly recognisable, owing to the number of years it has been left exposed in the dampest corner of the Atrium. There were present at this remarkable discovery, which took place at 6.30 A.M. on February 9, only four people besides the workmen, — the Crown Prince of Prussia, afterward the Emperor Frederick II., Dr. Henzen, one of my colleagues, and myself; and I distinctly remember how the prince, then in the full vigour of health and strength, helped the workmen to raise the masses of marble and to set the statues up against the wall of the atrium. That was the golden age of Roman excavation, and we recall it as if it were a dream! These beautiful statues had been piled into a regular oblong, like a cord of wood, by some diggers of marbles, who had carefully filled the spaces between the statues as they lay side by side, in order that no empty spaces might be left. By what fortunate accident these sculptures were preserved it is difficult to guess; but one thing at least is certain — a great quantity of other marbles belonging to the House of the Vestals must have perished by fire. Two kilns and two deposits of lime and of charcoal were found in the course of the same excavations.[1]

[1] See *Notizie degli Scavi*, December, 1883, p. 54.

CHAPTER XVII

THE BEGINNINGS OF THE MODERN CITY

In the fourteenth century Rome was still mediaeval; in the fifteenth it began to be slowly transformed into a modern city. While the seat of the papacy was at Avignon (1305-1377), three-quarters of the space within the walls was put under cultivation. The inhabitants, stricken with fever and poverty, lived like their prehistoric ancestors in mud huts with thatched roofs, and quenched their thirst with the waters of the Tiber. We are told that in the year 1377, on the return of Gregory XI. from Avignon, there were only 17,000 people in the entire area. Whether the figure is exact or not, the men who remained faithful to their native soil deserve the gratitude of mankind. Without them the site of Rome, completely deserted, might now have to be pointed out to the inquiring stranger as that of Veii, of Fidenae, of Ostia, and of Tusculum.

In the abandoned parts of the City a remnant of life could be found in the churches and fortified monasteries of the Caelian, Esquiline, and Aventine hills, as that of S. Balbina, which retained its mediaeval character until its "modernisation" in 1884. Vines and olive trees grew in the halls of the imperial palace on the Palatine, and cattle grazed again on the site of the Forum, as in the days of Evander. Here and there stood the dismantled ruins of baronial houses destroyed by the victor of the day; other quarters — the Campo Torrecchiano, for instance — were bristling with square brick towers, loopholed and battlemented, obtrusive proof of perpetual warfare and bloodshed. The strongholds of the Normanni, Papi, Romani, Stefaneschi, Anicii, and Anguillara dominated the region of Trastevere, while those of the Pierleoni commanded the entrance to the Ponte di Santa Maria (the ancient Pons Aemilius, now Ponte Rotto), and those of the Frangipani the island of S. Bartolomeo (Fig. 34).

The ruins of the amphitheatre of Statilius Taurus (Monte Giordano), and of Pompey's theatre (Campo di Fiori), were in the hands of the Orsini. The Savelli had supplanted the Pierleoni in the possession of the theatre of Marcellus (Monte Savello). The Colonna family occupied a fortified enclosure in the abandoned quarter about Trajan's Forum, with the centre of their stronghold at the temple of the Sun on the Quirinal (Villa Colonna), while the mausoleum of Augustus and the hill of Monte Citorio, strongly garrisoned, were utilised by them as detached forts. One of their towers, at the corner of the Via Tre Cannelli and Via Nazionale, is still standing; there are also towers of the Mellini and Sanguigni near the Stadium, of the Sinibaldi and

Crescenzi near the Pantheon. These ugly square structures were raised to protect the residences of the barons, which had not the aspect of a palace, but of a cluster

FIG. 34.— House and tower of the Margani.

of low, narrow dwellings, enclosed by a battlemented wall. Around them lived the vassals and partisans, who every night barred with chains the surrounding lanes. The great fortress of the Frangipani covered the southern half of the Palatine, the core of the fortification being the Septizonium; and this family had outposts also at the Coliseum, at the Turris Cartularia, at the Janus Quadrifrons of the Forum Boarium, and at the arches of Titus and Constantine.

The great Torre de' Conti, erected by Nicholas I. about 858, and rebuilt by Innocent III. in 1216, was called by Petrarch *Turris toto orbe unica* from its prodigious height and strength. It commanded the district of the Carinae and of the Subura. The upper part having collapsed during the earthquake of 1348, Pope Urban VIII. pulled down the rest, as far as the top of the lowest of the three stories. Much better preserved is the Torre delle Milizie, the construction of which was popularly attributed to Nero. It was very likely built by Pandolfo della Suburra in 1210. In the second half of the same century it became the property of the Annibaldi, and later passed into the possession of the Caetani.

The aspect of Rome in those days may be compared with that of S. Geminiano to-day. In many parts there were towers crowned with battlements and with iron brackets for signal fires (Fig. 35). Their number was so great that a district of the City on the slopes and at the foot of the Oppian hill was actually called the Campo Torrecchiano.

All sense of the beautiful, all appreciation of art,

FIG. 35. — A lane of mediaeval Rome — Via della Lungarina, demolished in 1877.

seems to have been lost for a time among the Romans. While other cities in Italy were raising churches, town halls, exchanges, fountains, palaces, and splendid private houses which command admiration at the present day on account of the graceful simplicity of their proportions and the finish of their work, the builders at Rome did little more than pile up and jumble together fragments of older structures, without regard to form or fitness. Tivoli, Viterbo, and even Corneto, were in this period far superior to Rome in their public and domestic architecture. They can point to splendid examples of the skill and taste of their master masons of the fourteenth century, while we Romans have absolutely nothing to show that is comparable. Every trace of the local influence of the Cosmatesque School seems to have disappeared before the beginning of the fifteenth century. When, therefore, interest in artistic construction began to revive, as the handicrafts which form the auxiliaries of art no longer existed in the City, artisans from other parts of Italy, especially from Tuscany, Umbria, and the region of the lakes of Como and Lugano, had to be summoned to Rome.

The first impulse toward the rebuilding of the City was given by Eugene IV., who occupied the chair of St. Peter from 1431 to 1447. A splendid memorial of Paul II. (1464–1471) is the palace of St. Mark, now called Palazzo Venezia. Under the pontificates of Paul's successors, Sixtus IV., Innocent VIII. (1484–1492), and

Alexander VI. (1492-1503), Baccio Pontelli carried to Rome the artistic traditions of Brunelleschi, and erected successively the churches of S. Maria del Popolo, S. Pietro in Montorio, S. Agostino, S. Maria della Pace, the Sistine chapel, the façades of S. Pietro in Vincoli and of the SS. Apostoli, the hospital of S. Spirito, the palace of the Governo Vecchio, and the great court of the pontifical palace, near the church of S. Maria Maggiore, which was recently destroyed. To Bramante we owe the beautiful court of S. Damaso in the Vatican, the Belvedere, the galleries connecting this last with the pontifical residence, the round temple in the cloisters of S. Pietro in Montorio, and the palaces of the Riario (now the Cancelleria) and of Cardinal di Corneto, now Torlonia-Giraud.

The aspect of the City was considerably changed by the erection of these buildings. Early in the fifteenth century the modern spirit, so methodical in all things and so fond of straight lines, began to manifest itself in the cutting of spacious streets through the ruins and rambling habitations of the City. By a bull dated March 30, 1425, Martin V. reëstablished the office of the commissioners of streets (*magistri viarum*). Eugene IV. straightened and paved several of the lanes in the Campus Martius; Nicholas V. the Via di S. Celso (now Via de' Banchi); and Paul II. paved the Corso between the Arco di Portogallo near S. Lorenzo in Lucina, and the Piazza Venezia. Sixtus IV. was named "the great builder" (*gran fabbricatore*), on account of the many improvements made under his rule; and Alexander VI. carried the Via Alexandrina through the Borgo.

It cannot be denied that these improvements in the material aspect and welfare of the City involved great losses on the archaeological and historical side. Without entering into particulars regarding the extent of the transformation, which will be fully given in my volumes on the *Storia degli Scavi di Roma*, it will be sufficient for our purpose to follow Poggio Bracciolini in his ride through the City in 1447, the year of the election of Nicholas V. Beginning with the Capitol, Poggio describes the southern platform of the hill, where the Caffarelli palace now stands, as covered with the colossal remains of the temple of Jupiter; but a few decades later columns, capitals, and frieze had disappeared so completely that archaeologists since then have found serious difficulty in determining which of the two summits of the hill was occupied by the Capitolium and which by the Citadel. Speaking of the temple of Isis and Serapis, near the church of La Minerva, Poggio mentions two interesting particulars. He says that a local gardener in planting a tree had lately discovered a head of one of the colossal river-gods, which, together with other recumbent figures, once lined the dromos of the temple, but being annoyed by the curiosity of the people, who rushed to see his find, at once covered it up again. He also speaks of the remains of a portico with many columns, either lying on the ground or half buried under the ruins of the temple. Some of these columns were removed in December, 1451, to the Loggia of the Benediction at St. Peter's, under the skilful management of the engineer from Bologna, Maestro Aristotile di Fioravante degli Alberti.

Of the temple of Concord, Poggio says that when he first visited Rome in 1431 the front portico, facing the Forum, was almost intact; but that later the whole temple with a part of the portico was destroyed. Similar instances of wanton destruction are recorded by him in the case of portions of the Coliseum, as well as of the remains at Ostia and other suburban places.

The general practice followed by these fifteenth century builders, whether popes, cardinals, patricians, or simple citizens, was this: Before commencing their work they would secure the possession of a *petraia*, that is, an ancient structure or part of a structure, from which they could obtain materials of construction, lime and ornamental marbles. There is no edifice in Rome dating from the fifteenth century the erection of which did not simultaneously carry with it the destruction or the mutilation of some ancient structure. I add a few instances.

When Martin V., in July, 1425, undertook the laying of the beautiful cosmatesque pavement of St. John Lateran, Antonio Picardi and Nicolao Bellini, contractors for the work, received the Pope's permission to strip of their marbles all the churches, "both within and without the City," in which divine service was no longer celebrated. Apparently the contractors gave to the grant a very broad interpretation, and laid hands not only on abandoned places of worship, but on the very tomb of the prince of the apostles. In a brief of March 29, 1436, Eugene IV. complains that some precious slabs of porphyry and serpentine had been wrenched off from the pontifical chair, which was, as it were, "the altar of the most blessed Peter!" The same Pope issued a second brief for the protection of the Coliseum against the "diggers of marbles"; and yet I find that stones from the Coliseum were used by him in the restoration of the apse of St. John Lateran, and marbles from the Curia and the Forum Julium in the restoration of the Apostolic palace.

The monuments which suffered the most under the rule of Nicholas V. are the Coliseum, the Circus Maximus, the Curia, and the temple of Venus and Rome. A document of 1452[1] certifies that one contractor alone, Giovanni Paglia Lombardo, was allowed to remove from the Coliseum 2522 cartloads of travertine in the space of only nine months. The temple of Venus and Rome was worked as a quarry from 1450 to 1454, the porphyry columns of both cellae being used as lining for the lime-kilns on account of their refractory qualities. The same Pope destroyed the triumphal arch of Gratian, Valen-

[1] Published by Müntz in *Revue Archéologique*, September, 1876.

tinian, and Theodosius, by the church of S. Celso in Banchi, in order to widen the Piazza di Ponte S. Angelo; and he built also the foundations of the two expiatory chapels at the entrance to the same bridge with statues and ornamental marbles from the mausoleum of Hadrian. In 1456 twenty blocks of rare marble were removed from Ostia to Orvieto and made use of in the decoration of the façade of the Duomo.

The building of the Loggia of the Benediction at St. Peter's, the masterpiece of the time of Pius II., caused more damage to ancient monuments than a barbaric invasion. Materials were extracted and lime obtained from the Coliseum, the temple of Jupiter Capitolinus, the Forum Julium, the Senate-house, the bridge of Nero, the Palatiolum on the hill of S. Spirito, the temple of the Dea Dia on the Via Campana, the portico of Octavia, the Baths of Caracalla, the templum Sacrae Urbis (SS. Cosma e Damiano), the ruins of Ostia, the Milvian bridge, and the massive tombs of the Via Flaminia near the farmhouses of Valca and Valchetta. The next Pope, Paul II., built the palace of St. Mark with the spoils of the temple of Claudius on the Caelian, of the Coliseum, of a temple near S. Maria in Cosmedin, of the tombs of the Via Flaminia, of the Septa Julia, and of an unknown travertine building (the Gaianum?) in the vineyard of the banker Tommaso Spinelli; and he raised the beautiful Castello at Tivoli with materials taken from the Amphitheatre. Nevertheless, the genial

Aeneas Silvio Piccolomini issued his famous brief of April 28, 1462, commencing, "*Cum almam nostram urbem*," in which he threatened heavy penalties and the pontifical wrath against the destroyers of ancient remains.

Of Sixtus IV. we have two briefs that are important for our subject. One is dated December 17, 1471; it authorises "the architects of the Vatican library to make excavations anywhere in order to secure the stone

FIG. 36.—The Porta del Popolo of the time of Sixtus IV. From a sketch by M. Heemskerk (1536).

needed" for the work.[1] The other, dated April 7, 1474, inflicts "the greater excommunication" on those who remove marbles from "the patriarchal and other churches and basilicas." The beautiful round temple of Hercules Victor, the tutelary god of the charioteers of the circus, which stood near the Ara Maxima and the Forum Boarium, was one of the monuments destroyed under the rule of this pontiff. The two square towers on either side of the Porta del Popolo (Fig. 36) were built in the

[1] Müntz, *Les Arts à la cour des Papes*, Vol. III. p. 15.

same pontificate with marbles from the tombs of Aelius Gutta Calpurnianus, the famous charioteer (Fig. 37); of Lucius Nonius Asprenas, consul A.D. 6; of Valerius Nicias; of a patrician lady named Postuma, and from an unknown tomb of pyramidal shape which stood on the site of the present church of S. Maria de' Miracoli. Altogether 250 large marble blocks were used in the building of the two bastions.[1]

FIG. 37. — Reliefs from the tomb of Calpurnianus, the charioteer.

The list for this century closes with the destruction of a triumphal arch (called *arcus novus*) near S. Maria in Via Lata, the materials of which were used by Innocent VIII. in the restoration of this church, and the removal of the great pyramid of the Borgo — the so-called Meta Romuli[2] — which was accomplished by Alexander VI. in the widening and straightening of the Via Alexandrina. The same Pope built a round tower near the gate of the castle of S. Angelo with the marble frieze and veneering of Hadrian's mausoleum.

[1] Visconti in *Bull. Com.*, 1877, p. 185 *sq.*   [2] See p. 178.

Among the palaces built by private individuals during this century I shall mention only two, — the palace of Cardinal Adriano di Corneto, now Torlonia-Giraud, which was built with the spoils of the Basilica Julia and of the four-faced temple of Janus; and the Palazzo della Cancelleria, built by Cardinal Riario with stone from the Coliseum and with marbles from the triumphal arch of Gordianus, near the Praetorian camp.

Before passing to the disastrous sack of Rome by the army of Charles of Bourbon, I must remark that the first quarter of the sixteenth century showed a decided improvement in the increasing appreciation of the value of certain classes of ancient monuments on the part of such popes as Julius II. and Leo X., and such private individuals as Raphael and his archaeological advisers, Fabio Calvo da Ravenna and Andrea Fulvio. Statuary and inscriptions were especially prized. The finding of the Laocoon among the ruins of the house of Titus on the Oppian seems to have struck with amazement the Pope, the court, the artists, in fact the whole population. A general search for works of sculpture was afterward instituted, in the course of which the remains of old buildings suffered great damage. The science of topography was in its infancy, and the importance of preserving ancient buildings was slow to be recognised.

The last years of Alexander VI., who died in 1503, were marked by the destruction of a portion of the Baths of Diocletian, of an unknown temple on the Sacra Via, and of the Forum Transitorium.[1] Julius II., his successor (1503-1513), was too much absorbed in military operations to give much attention to the remains of ancient Rome. However, he took up in earnest the reconstruction of the Constantinian Basilica of St. Peter's. Since the time of Nicholas V. fears had been entertained for the safety of the building, and Leon Battista Alberti and Bernardo Rossellino had been commissioned to prepare plans for its reconstruction. The work was progressing very slowly when Julius II. gave it a new impulse, placing it under the direction of Bramante, who entered upon his duties in 1503.[2]

Bramante's design was to substitute for the old church, of a pure basilica type, an edifice in the form of a Greek cross, with a hexastyle portico in front, and an immense cupola over the centre supported by four great piers. Julius II. laid the foundations of the Greek cross in 1506 under the pier now called della Veronica. The four piers and the arches which spring from them were the only parts of the structure completed at the time of the Pope's death. The loss occasioned to art, history, and Christian antiquities by the destruction of the venerable basilica is simply incalculable. The west half of the greatest temple of Christendom was levelled to the ground with all its precious decorations in mosaic, fresco, sculpture,

[1] *Jahrbuch für Kunst und Wiss.*, Vol. IV. p. 70.

[2] Curiously enough, the old St. Peter's appears in Jenichen's Panoramic View of Rome, engraved more than half a century later (*Frontispiece*).

in marble and in wood, with its historical inscriptions and its pontifical tombs, among which were those of Celestine IV. († 1243), Gregory IX. († 1241), Boniface IX. († 1404), Innocent VII. († 1406), Eugene IV. († 1447), and Nicholas V. († 1455).

Three other churches also disappeared in the pontificate of Julius II.: the old titulus Marcelli, which collapsed on the night of May 23, 1509; the church of S. Donatus, demolished for the opening of the Via Giulia; and the church of SS. Celso e Giuliano in Banchi, which was destroyed to widen the Piazza di Ponte.

No great losses are recorded under the rule of Leo X., who, on September 2, 1517, issued a bull, written in classic language, for the encouragement of those who might be willing to raise new edifices, "to the end that the City of Rome might increase in size and in dignity by reason of additions to its buildings and its population." The Via di Ripetta and the Via d' Aracoeli were opened by the same pontiff. The only act of vandalism which can be brought home to him is the destruction of a certain part of the Via Tiburtina, called La Quadrata, the embankment of which was supported by great walls of travertine. The stones were removed to St. Peter's.

CHAPTER XVIII

THE SACKING OF ROME BY THE ARMY OF CHARLES OF BOURBON IN 1527

THE sacking of Rome in 1527 was a calamity comparable only with the burning of the City by the Gauls in 390 B.C., and the destruction caused by the Normans in 1084.

One of the familiar lullabies sung to-day over the cradles of restless children begins with the words: "Fatti la ninna, è passa via Barbone! "Go to sleep, Barbone is gone," the name Barbone, "the man with the long beard," having usurped that of the hated conqueror. So persistent is the memory of those days of terror!

Charles of Bourbon, the remorseless leader of a cruel army, appeared before the crumbling walls of the Leonine City May 5, 1527, and placed his headquarters in the convent of S. Onofrio, opposite the gate of S. Spirito (Fig. 38). Although he himself fell the victim of a stray shot early on the following day, his forces, comprising twenty thousand Germans, fourteen thousand Italians, and six thousand Spaniards, succeeded in storming the Borgo while the Pope was seeking shelter in the castle of S. Angelo. The pillage of the City,

Fig. 38. — The hill of S. Onofrio, where Charles of Bourbon established his headquarters.

with unspeakable horrors, lasted eight days, from the 6th to the 14th of May. In so short a time the treasures collected in the Roman palaces, churches, and convents, during the lapse of centuries, were dispersed.

The sacred precincts of St. Peter's fared worse at the hands of the Catholic Spaniards and Lombards than they had at the hands of the Saracens in 846. The Spaniards searched every tomb. They stripped the corpse of Julius II. of its pontifical vestments; they gambled with their booty, and rested themselves by lying stretched out on the venerable altars; they used the chalices of marvellous mediaeval workmanship as drinking cups, in company with profligate women; and they stabled their horses in the aisles of the sanctuary, preparing their litters with precious manuscripts collected by Pius II. and Sixtus IV. The stained glass windows of Guillaume de Marcillat were broken into bits, and the Flemish tapestries designed by Raphael were stolen for the sake of their gold threads.

The fate of these world-famous tapestries is closely connected with that of the City, and throws light on the vicissitudes to which relics of antiquity in Rome have been exposed in these later centuries. Pope Leo X., thirteen years before these events, had given Raphael a commission to draw cartoons illustrating scenes from the New Testament. The cartoons were copied in tapestry by Bernhard van Orlay and

Michael Coxie, and the priceless fabrics thus produced were exhibited in the Sistine chapel on certain church festivals. The tapestries were stolen by the lansquenets, and were carried off with other spoils from the Vatican. In 1553, however, they came into the possession of Anne de Montmorency, who restored them to their legitimate owner; but some of them were lost forever.

Even the tapestries that had been preserved to this time were not to be spared further vicissitudes. They experienced perhaps a worse treatment in 1798 at the hands of the French invaders, when they were sold for a nominal sum to a Genoese Jew. He burnt one of them for the sake of the gold and silver threads, of which Van Orlay had made use in weaving the bright lights, but the profits did not meet his expectations. Pius VII. bought the rest back in 1808. During the siege of Rome in 1849 they were exposed to injury for the third time from General Oudinot's artillery. Two cannon-balls entered the gallery where the tapestries were hung; one fell on the floor, and the other burst directly in front of the one portraying the Miraculous Draught of Fishes.

If we recall the vast collections of objects of value which the piety of the faithful had heaped up in the sacristies of Roman churches during the preceding centuries, we can appreciate the losses of the month of May, 1527. Sacred vessels of small size were packed in sacks and carried off; others which could not be removed were destroyed, and the most precious relics were treated with contumely. The busts of St. Peter and of St. Paul, the head of St. Andrew,[1] and that of John the Presbyter were stolen respectively from their shrines in the Lateran, in the Vatican, and in the church of S. Silvestro in Capite. A German soldier hoisted on the point of his lance the spear which was believed to be the one with which Longinus had pierced the side of the Redeemer on the cross; it had been presented to Pope Innocent VII. by Bayazed II., and was preserved in the famous shrine of the Santa Lancia, a masterpiece of the school of Mino da Fiesole, destroyed by Paul V. in 1606. The vail, said to have belonged to St. Veronica, and to bear the impression of the Saviour's features, was dragged from tavern to tavern among the jeerings and taunts of the drunken soldiery.[2] The cross of Constantine, which hung over the Apostle's tomb in St. Peter's, was tossed in the mud of the Via di Borgo and trampled under

[1] The head of St. Andrew was stolen again in 1848 and hidden in a recess of the city walls between the Porta Cavalleggeri and the Porta S. Pancrazio. A marble statue erected by Pius IX. marks the spot where the relic was re-discovered in 1850.

[2] This relic, the first one which the pilgrims sought on their visit *ad limina*, was kept in a shrine built by John VII. The shrine was destroyed in 1606, together with its priceless mosaic pictures. The image of the Virgin alone was saved by Cardinal Pallotta, who made a present of it to the Ricci of Florence. It is now preserved in the chapel of that family in the church of S. Marco.

foot. Even the chapel of St. Lawrence in the Lateran palace, the most august shrine of the Catholic world, was profaned and stripped of all its contents.

Furniture, pictures, and works of art of every description were destroyed in private houses and palaces; pearls and precious stones were apportioned among the German mercenaries by spoonfuls, the share of an ordinary soldier in the booty being from three to four thousand ducats. Exquisite refinements of cruelty were devised to extort money from persons suspected of having concealed it. The old Cardinal Ponzetta, although a partisan of the Emperor, was held for a ransom of twenty thousand ducats, and afterward dragged through the streets of the City with his hands tied behind him; he died soon after in great destitution. Another cardinal, Cristoforo Numalio, was torn from the bed where he was lying ill, placed on a hearse, and dragged in procession in his ecclesiastical robes. Drunken soldiers and profligate women surrounded the bier, brandishing torches and vociferating infamous songs in imitation of priestly canticles. Thus the unfortunate old man was carried into the church of the Aracoeli and lowered into a crypt, to be buried alive unless a fresh ransom should be paid. Friends came to his rescue at the last moment.

Still more unhappy was the fate of a priest whose name ought to be enrolled in the list of heroes. A group of drunken soldiers had dressed a donkey in sacerdotal robes and made it kneel before a street shrine. Having caught hold of a priest, they tried to force him to administer the holy communion to the brute. The good old man, to save the Host from such profanation, swallowed it before they could prevent him, and suffered from those demons in human flesh one of the most horrible martyrdoms recorded in the history of persecutions. The loss sustained by the City in those eventful days has been valued at seven or eight million of ducats by Scaramuccia Trivulzio, cardinal of Como; at fifteen by Ulloa, the biographer of Charles V.; while Gregorovius, in estimating this loss, mentions a sum of twenty millions of florins — nearly a million and a half pounds sterling, or between seven and eight millions of dollars.

In the light of these barbarities, it is not surprising to find that Giovio, Cappella, Brantôme, and others assert that many ancient statues, the work of Greek chisels, were mutilated or destroyed; that Raphael's frescoes in the Stanze and those of Pinturicchio in the Sale Borgia of the Vatican were deliberately injured by the smoke of bonfires lighted in the middle of the halls; that the very tomb of St. Peter, deep under the apse of the Constantinian Basilica, was broken into, and the remains of the Apostle scattered to the four winds; but these statements, if not altogether incorrect, are at least exaggerated.

We have quite definite information regarding the number and the quality of the statues discovered and exhibited in Roman palaces and villas before 1527. Chief among them were the recumbent colossal figures of the Nile and of the Tiber, found at the time of Leo X. among the ruins of the temple of Isis; the Commodus with the attributes of Hercules (Heracles and Telephos), found on May 15, 1507, in the Piazza di Campo di Fiori and removed to the Belvedere gardens by Julius II.; a torso of Heracles in the possession of the Colonnas; another — the torso of the Belvedere — discovered in 1513 under the Ciampolini house at the Campo di Fiori, and removed to the Vatican by Clement VII.; the Sleeping Ariadne, whose place of discovery is not known; the Belvedere Apollo, found, not at Antium, as is usually stated, but on a farm of Cardinal Giuliano della Rovere, near Grotta Ferrata; and the Laocoon group, found on January 14, 1506, by Felice de Fredis in his vineyard on the Oppian hill. There were also the bronze works of art presented to the Senate and Roman people by Sixtus IV. and exhibited in the Palazzo dei Conservatori; the statue of Marcus Aurelius, now on the Capitoline hill; the marble horse-tamers, the three Constantines, and the two river-gods of the Quirinal.

All these marbles and bronzes have come down to us uninjured except one, the Heracles of the Colonna palace, which has disappeared; and the frescoes of Raphael, as well as those of Pinturicchio, are still to be seen. In examining these last, when the Sale Borgia were reopened three years ago by order of Leo XIII., I observed German names scratched with a pointed instrument, whether a sword or knife I could not tell, on the lower surface of the wall; but whether they are names of the mercenaries of Charles V. or of more peaceful visitors of later times I am unable to say (Fig. 39).

FIG. 39. — One of the Sale Borgia — that of the " Vita della Madonna " — in the Vatican.

Reissner asserts that the right arm of the central figure of the Laocoon group must have been broken off after it was discovered; but it is a fact quite generally known that the arm was missing at the time of discovery. The assertion of a letter published some years ago by

I. Mayerhofer in the *Historisches Jahrbuch* (1891, p. 751) that the tomb of St. Peter was violated during the sack of 1527, has been distinctly contradicted by Grisar.[1] The letter was written by Theodoric Vafer (alias Gescheid), and bears the date of June 17, 1527. "The soldiers," the writer says, "have profaned every church in Rome, and have slaughtered their victims on the altars of the apostles; they have broken the coffins, or urns, containing the relics of St. Peter and St. Paul, and dispersed the precious dust; they have stolen the sacred vessels used in the divine service," etc. Professor Grisar thinks that we ought not to take too literally the expressions of a man writing under the excitement of the appalling disaster; certainly not one of the hundreds of descriptions by eye-witnesses of the events agrees with this statement.

Interesting discoveries have from time to time been made in connexion with this sack of the City.

A diarist of the last century, named Cecconi, relates that in 1705 a treasure of sixty thousand scudi was found in the cellars of the Palazzo Verospi on the Corso, where it had been concealed in 1527. Again, on the morning of June 1, 1879, an apprentice mason engaged in repairing the drain of a house at No. 23, Via della Stelletta, found a shiny piece of metal, and put it in his pocket waiting for a chance to show it to a connoisseur. In the meanwhile the dirt from the drain

[1] See *Le tombe Apostoliche di Roma*, Roma, 1892, p. 27, n. 40.

was carted away in the direction of the Porta Angelica. The lad was caught in the act of receiving twenty francs for his piece from a goldsmith opposite. Search was made at once on the spot, and 142 gold coins were found in and near the drain. Policemen were sent after the carts. They overtook these outside the Porta Angelica, examined the contents, and found forty-two more pieces, to the great amazement of the drivers, who had no idea that they were removing gold from such an unexpected mine. One hundred and eighty-four gold pieces had therefore been concealed in the drain of the house during or immediately before the pillage of 1527. The date is certain: the coins bear the effigy, the coat of arms, and the legend of Pius II., who died in 1464; of Innocent VIII., who died in 1492; of Alexander VI., who died in 1503; and of other predecessors of Clement VII., under whose pontificate the pillage took place. The coins of Clement VII. himself amount to one-third of the whole number.[1]

The hiding-place of chief importance is the bed of the Tiber; for, rather than allow their treasures to be seized by the invaders, the Romans threw their valuables into the arms of Father Tiber, who gathered them in his muddy treasury, and has preserved them to our day.

---

[1] At the time of the discovery it was asserted that a coin with the effigy and name of Paul III. had been seen in the treasure-trove, a fact that, if substantiated, would place the concealment of this gold at a later period than the sack. I have not been able to see the coin in question.

When, in 1877, the works connected with the construction of the embankments along the river and the widening and deepening of its bed began, I made it a point to ascertain the comparative depth of the various finds with a view to determining the stratification of the objects of every description at the bottom. The task was not easy, because more dredgers were kept at work and more compressed-air caissons were sunk at the same time than one could watch personally, and, in such delicate inquiries, personal observation is necessary.

Comparing the notes taken from 1878 to 1889, I have come to the following result: that if we leave out of account the miscellaneous objects which may pertain to any age and hence are not conclusive, the archaeological strata of the Tiber correspond with considerable regularity to the leading catastrophes in the history of Rome. The objects with which the dredgers first came into contact recall the revolution of 1848-1849, and bear witness to the haste with which compromising objects, as republican symbols and weapons of every kind, were made to disappear as soon as General Oudinot had become the master of the City. The next important layer seems to correspond with the French invasion of 1798-1799; and the third from the top yields as its harvest innumerable mementoes of the sack of Charles of Bourbon.

CHAPTER XIX

THE MONUMENTS IN THE LATTER PART OF THE SIXTEENTH CENTURY

THE wretched state of Rome in the latter part of the sixteenth century is hardly concealed beneath the superficial brilliancy of the Renaissance. The following facts, which I have gathered at random from contemporary records, cast light upon the condition of things.

In April, 1566, Pius V. directed the cardinals Crispo, di Montepulciano, and Sforza "to see that the streets of Rome are promptly cleaned, so that when the heat of summer comes the air shall not be tainted." Apparently, no attempt to clean the streets had been made for years. As the country roads were only repaired four times each century, in the years of Jubilee, so the streets were only cleaned on great occasions, as when a newly elected pope rode in state to the Lateran to take possession of his chair. To illustrate another aspect of the administration, I may mention the curious means adopted by Pius IV. and the City government to diminish vagrancy. They determined that "the magistrates at the head of the thirteen wards of the City, accompanied by thirteen gentlemen chosen by the Council — one for each region — should go around their parishes once a month with the almsbox" (July 8, 1562). The feast of the Birth-day of Rome, the glorious Palilia, on the twenty-first of April, was no longer celebrated, for lack of money, but in 1549 a revival was proposed on the ground that "some gentlemen had said that they were willing to contribute from their private purse" to defray the expenses of the celebration.

In justice to the City magistrates of this period, we must acknowledge that, so far as relates to the preservation of the ancient monuments, their behaviour was very different from that of the popes and of the Apostolic Chamber. While the papal authorities had officially sanctioned and encouraged the destruction of classic remains, particularly by a bull of Paul III. dated July 22, 1540, the municipal officials never ceased to raise their voice in favour of their preservation, and to protest against the shameful deeds of the commissioners for the "Fabbrica di S. Pietro." Their love and reverence for the *alma parens* was never crushed by untoward events. This attitude of mind was so consistent and unvarying that in the many hundred volumes of Records which I have consulted in the municipal archives, I have found no trace of any opposition to projects connected with the safeguarding of the classic remains, or with the increase of the archaeological collections of the Capitoline Museum. On the

FIG. 40.— Bas-reliefs from the arch of Marcus Aurelius, removed from the church of S. Martina in 1525, now in the Conservatori Palace.

THE MONUMENTS IN THE SIXTEENTH CENTURY 231

contrary, regard for the glories of the past was at times carried to an extreme, and the City Council now and then transformed itself, as it were, into an academy of humanists. Even allowing that this overzealous devotion to antiquity might justly be criticised, we are compelled to admire the patriotism of the City officials, for in the cause of art they forgot all else — present trials, gloomy prospects for the future, and sometimes, also, we must confess, the sense of justice; thus in March, 1525, they took away from the rector of the church of S. Martina the bas-reliefs from the arch of Marcus Aurelius,[1] now on the landing of the staircase of the Conservatori Palace, without allowing him any compensation (Fig. 40).

In 1538, after 320 scudi had been laboriously collected from the Cerrini and other defaulters and criminals in the district of Cori, the City Council voted that "of the said sum of 320 scudi a portion should be devoted to the setting up of the equestrian statue of M. Antonius (*sic*), according to the design of Master Michael Angelo, sculptor, and another portion to the building of the substruction walls of the Piazza del Campidoglio." The equestrian statue referred to is the bronze Marcus Aurelius which was then set up in the square of the Capitol, where it has remained ever since. In the Middle Ages it had stood near the Lateran (Fig. 42); and its preservation is thought to have been

[1] *C. I. L.* VI. 1014.

due to the belief that it was a statue of Constantine, the first Christian Emperor.

The interest of the municipal authorities in the preservation of statuary is illustrated also by the following incident. When Pius IV., in 1561, urged the Municipality to complete in timber the unfinished portion of the bridge of Santa Maria (now called the Ponte Rotto), the Council hesitated to accept the suggestion until Monsignor Rufino guaranteed " to reimburse the Municipality in the sum of 2000 scudi if the plan should not succeed." It happened that the repairs were not successful, and the City commenced proceedings against Monsignor Rufino for reimbursement of the money. After paying 640 scudi, he asked the City to accept in settlement of the balance due them " two beautiful statues," to be valued by experts, for the decoration of the new Capitoline buildings. The proposal was accepted, and Mario Frangipani and Tommaso de' Cavalieri were appointed appraisers with power to choose a third appraiser to assist them. The statues are still to be seen, on either side of the vestibule of the Conservatori Palace. They are colossal in size, both found, according to a somewhat doubtful tradition, in the Forum Julium. The one on the right represents Julius Caesar; that on the left, a victorious Roman admiral.

In December, 1584, the restoration of the colossal statues of Castor and Pollux came to a standstill on account of the lack of funds. In order to provide the means to complete the work the Council farmed out the office of public notary for two of the wards of the City,

FIG. 41. — The statues of Castor and Pollux on the Capitoline hill, restored in 1584.

the Rione di Ripa and the Curia Capitolina, and the statues were set in the places which they now occupy (Fig. 41).

In 1576, in spite of the emptying of the treasury to

defray the expenses of the Jubilee of 1575, the City fathers voted a large sum, for those days, to bring the dispute regarding the possession of the *Lex Regia* to a satisfactory conclusion. This famous document is a copy, engraved in bronze, of the decree by which the "Senate and the Roman people" conferred the imperial power on Vespasian. The tablet had been used by Boniface VIII. in the construction of an altar in St. John Lateran, and set so awkwardly that it could hardly be read. Cola di Rienzi, in 1346, caused it to be taken from its hiding-place and set up in the nave, where, showing it to his fellow-citizens, he was wont to speak fiery words on the right of the people to choose their own form of government. The efforts of the municipality to secure the valuable document had always failed, owing to the opposition of the Canons of the Lateran. Compelled at last by a decree of the Pope to take some action, the Canons voted to commit the precious tablet to the guardian care of "the Roman people," and as they begged that they might receive something in return, the Council, out of gratitude, gave them 200 gold scudi on condition that they purchase a silver ewer and basin and a pair of candelabra for use in the basilica. The 200 scudi were secured by pawning certain objects of value belonging to the City.

In the minutes of the City Council for May 17, 1580, I find the following statement: "It is clearly seen that the antiquities of Rome are disappearing every day, on account of the search for marbles, which is carried on in the most reckless manner, with no regard to the preservation of the ruins themselves. We have a recent instance of this in the Palazzo Maggiore (the palace of the Caesars) where the most beautiful halls have been undermined so as to require new foundations and buttresses to be kept standing." A deputation was sent to Pope Gregory XIII., instructed to ask him to revoke all grants given by the Apostolic Chamber "for the procuring of marble and travertine from the ancient ruins of the City, even for the Fabbrica di S. Pietro and the church of the Prince of the Apostles." The result of this interview may be inferred from the fact that by another apostolic brief the destructive powers of the Fabbrica di S. Pietro were extended to the ruins of Ostia and Porto.

In the Autobiography of Cardinal Giovanni Antonio Santori, edited by Professor Cugnoni,[1] a characteristic instance is given of the way that Sixtus V. dealt with ancient monuments. "Seeing that the Pope was quite bent on the destruction of the antiquities of Rome," says the Cardinal, "many Roman noblemen came to beg me to try to persuade his Holiness to abandon his strange purpose, particularly as he cherished the intention of destroying the Septizonium (as he afterward did), the Velabrum (that is, the four-faced arch of the Forum

[1] See Vol. XII. p. 372, and Vol. XIII. p. 151, of the *Archivio della Società reale di Storia patria.*

Boarium), and the Capo di Bove," which we know as the tomb of Caecilia Metella, that rare and splendid monument of the Republic. "I made this request in company with Cardinal Colonna, and received the reply that he wished to remove the unsightly ruins in order to repair those that required it." And indeed, in May, 1589, Giovanni Battista Mottino and Girolamo Leni and his brothers had no difficulty in obtaining permission from Cardinal di Montalto, the Pope's Camarlingo, to pull down the mausoleum of Caecilia Metella. The rescript, however, contained a provision: "Our Sovereign Lord and Master grants the concession, provided that the Roman people are content." This clause saved the monument, as I will show; but I think it worth while to give here the exact words of the request made to the Pope, so characteristic is it of the spirit of the age : —

"Gio. Battista Mottino, and Girolamo Leni and his brothers, are the owners of the farm-lands of Capo di Bove, where there is a tomb, or tower, which it would be very advantageous to them to dismantle. They therefore humbly pray your Holiness that they may be granted permission in such a way that the gentlemen of the City Council (Signori Conservatori) cannot oppose it by saying it is an antiquity, which they ought not to say, as it is out of Rome and not in a public place, and others have been dismantled, one on the road to Tivoli, another of marble at Ponte dell'

Arco, yet another at Casal Rotonno, and many others.[1] If your Holiness will make this concession we think that the Roman people (popolo Romano) will do likewise to please him, and thus all we receive will be by the special favour of our Master, and we will unceasingly pray God for his preservation, and that a long and happy life be granted to your Excellency."

The "popolo Romano," on whom Cardinal di Montalto had sought to lay the responsibility, at first hesitated, and the work of demolition began, but so numerous and serious were the remonstrances that, on the motion of Paolo Lancellotti, seconded by his colleagues, Ottavio Gabrielli, and Alessandro Gottifredi, the Municipal Council cancelled the permission, and so the tomb of Metella was saved. This occurrence, and others of the same nature, possibly account for the change of feeling among the people toward Sixtus V. Those same magistrates who had ordered the erection of a statue to him, November 26, 1585, to commemorate the return of peace and plenty, thus announce the death of the Pope to the Council on Monday, August 24, 1590: "To-day, our most Holy Lord, Pope

[1] I cannot quite make out which tomb on Via Tiburtina is alluded to in this petition of Mottino and his friends; perhaps it is that described in Cod. Vat. 3439, f. 35. The *antiquità al ponte dell' Arco* is the tomb of M. Antonius Antius Lupus, about which see *Bull. Com.*, 1891, p. 221. The mausoleum of Aurelius Cotta still bears the characteristic name given it in the memorial (Casal Rotondo).

Sixtus V., has departed this life, amidst the rejoicings and mutual congratulations of all classes of citizens."[1]

But Sixtus V. was great in everything, in his friendship and in his enmity, in his modesty and in his magnificence, in the benefits he conferred on the Eternal City, and in the contempt he professed toward the classic ruins. It would, perhaps, be more correct to say toward some classic ruins, for we cannot forget that, in spite of so many acts of destruction, we owe to him the restoration of the columns of Trajan and of Marcus Aurelius, and of the Horse-tamers of the Quirinal, the discovery and reërection of three obelisks, the removal of the Vatican obelisk to a more suitable place, and the renovation of the whole City.

The demolition of the Septizonium of Septimius Severus took place in the winter of 1588–1589, under the direction of the Pope's favourite architect, Domenico Fontana. Some 905 scudi were expended in the work, but the valuable materials recovered, blocks of peperino and travertine, and columns of rare marbles, more than offset the expenditure. It is interesting to see what became of the spoils of this famous building, the loss of which archaeologists have regretted more than of almost any other in Rome.

"Thirty-three blocks of stone," I have stated elsewhere, "were used in the foundation of the pedestal of

[1] *Hodie sanctissimus dominus noster, Syxtus papa quintus, omnibus congratulantibus et maxima omnium laetitia, diem suum clausit extremum.*

the obelisk in the Piazza del Popolo; 104 of marble in the restoration of the column of Marcus Aurelius, including the base of the bronze statue of St. Paul; 15 in the tomb of the Pope in the Cappella del Presepio, at S. Maria Maggiore, and an equal number in that of Pius V. The staircase of the Casa dei Mendicanti, or workhouse, by the Ponte Sisto, and that of the Trinità de' Monti, the wash-house (*lavatore*) in the Baths of Diocletian, the door of the Palazzo della Cancelleria; the north façade of St. John Lateran, the court and staircases of the adjoining palace, the fountain of the Moses on the Quirinal, and lastly, the church of S. Girolamo degli Schiavoni, all had their share of the spoils of the Septizonium."[1]

The Baths of Diocletian were not more mercifully treated; Gualtieri, one of the Pope's admirers, sings the praises of the destruction of a portion of them (February 12, 1588). "We had," he says, "this large tract of land," the present Piazza di Termini, "which was of no use because uneven and covered with the ruins of the baths"; but now, thanks to Sixtus V., "it has been cleared and levelled up." Not less than 2,660,000 cubic feet of masonry were broken up in the course of the work. The figures can be verified in the pontifical Books of Account, from which we learn that the destruction lasted from May 16, 1586, to May 15 of the following year. The materials were carted

[1] *Ruins and Excavations*, p. 183.

away and put to use in raising the level of the Vicus Patricius (Via del Bambino Gesù), of the Vicus Portae Viminalis (Via Strozzi), and other adjacent streets.

Next in importance come the damages inflicted in the time of Sixtus V. upon the Claudian aqueduct, the arches of which, seven miles long, reached in places the height of one hundred and twenty feet above the level of the Campagna. Many of them were demolished that the materials might be used in the construction of the new Felice Aqueduct, which received its name from that of the Pope, Felice Peretti. As we have seen, the Claudian, the Marcian, the Alexandrine, and other aqueducts, had suffered little at the hands of the barbarians, who merely attempted to create a water famine in the besieged city by removing a few stones from the channels. The Marcian and Claudian aqueducts at any rate were practically intact till near the end of the sixteenth century. Upon Matteo da Castello and Domenico Fontana, the architects of Sixtus V., and upon the trustees of the hospital of S. Giovanni, rests the main part of the responsibility for their disappearance. Whenever the hospital was in need of money or building materials, a certain number of arches were sold by public auction, and demolished by the purchaser. I have found several grants in the archives of this charitable institution, conveying the right to destroy one, two, and even four, pilasters at one time.[1]

[1] See p. 85 and Fig. 20.

Some of the ruins, which are now the pride of the City, escaped destruction by a hair's breadth under the rule of this energetic Pope. One, as I have already intimated, is the so-called Janus Quadrifrons of the Forum Boarium. In a letter addressed to his architect, Fontana, dated January 4, 1588, Sixtus says: "I give you permission to destroy that ancient arch by S. Giorgio in Velabro, that you may use its marbles for the pedestal of the obelisk which I have resolved to erect in the Piazza del Laterano, and also for the coat of arms and the inscription which belong to the same pedestal. I grant you also the three columns of portasanta which support the portico of a canon's residence, near the Loggia of the Benediction, and the pieces of a fourth, which are lying there on the ground. These you are to use for the ciborium of our chapel in S. Maria Maggiore."

Fontana did not avail himself fully of the permission, being perhaps afraid to engage in acts, the vandalism of which was too obvious; and he took the precaution to provide himself with a safe-conduct from the Pope, which he could use in case the "Roman People" should arrest him. In another letter, dated February 5, 1589, the Pope says: "You are authorised to excavate, seize, and remove from any place you think it expedient, columns, marbles, travertine, and any other material necessary for the building and ornamentation of the chapel, which our sister, Donna Camilla, is adding to the church of S. Susanna. We give these materials as a present to her, and it is our will that no one shall interfere with you in the execution of our commands."

The aim which Sixtus had in view may be urged in extenuation of his treatment of the ancient monuments. We should not forget that while destroying with one hand ruins which, to his mind, had no value, he was with the other raising structures which to this day command the admiration of the world. We may freely concede that the loss of portions of the ancient aqueducts, for example, is fully compensated by the construction of the Acqua Felice, by means of which the higher parts of the Esquiline, Quirinal, and Pincian hills, almost entirely abandoned for eleven centuries on account of the dearth of water, were again made habitable.

There is, however, one act of vandalism that we can never forgive, — the destruction of the old Patriarchium, or pontifical residence at the Lateran, with its historic halls, chapels, oratories, banqueting rooms, loggias, colonnades, mosaic pictures, and inscriptions. It was the most wonderful museum of mediaeval art that ever existed. No one can read the accounts of Pompeo Ugonio and of Giacomo Grimaldi, without profound regret that so much of priceless value has been lost. The oratories of the Virgin Mary, dating from the time of Nicholas I. (858–867), of St. Sylvester and St. Sebastian, dating from the time of Theodore I. (642–

649), the church and monastery of St. Pancras, the shrines of S. Caesarius, of Michael the Archangel, of S. Apollinaris, dating from the time of Hadrian I. (772–795), the Leonine triclinium, the Loggia of the Benediction, built by Boniface VIII. (1300), the Council hall, —

FIG. 42. — View of the Lateran buildings before their destruction by Sixtus V. In the foreground (6), the bronze statue of Marcus Aurelius. From a sketch by Ciampini.

all were razed to the ground in a few months. The loss most lamented, not only by cultivated men of the day but also by the populace, was that of the Oratory of the Holy Cross (Oratorium Sanctae Crucis), the shape and location of which are shown in the sketch by Ciampini (Fig. 42).

This Oratory was in the form of a Greek cross, with a small atrium in front, surrounded on three sides by columns and presenting the type of a classic nymphaeum. There were three fountains of rare marble, one occupying the centre of the vestibule, the others at the sides, each with water trickling down into it from the capital of a column. The three doors were cast in bronze and inlaid with silver. Three of the four arms of the cross contained altars, while in the fourth stood the baptismal font. Exquisite mosaics adorned the ceiling, and the walls were covered with the finest marble veneering, of the sort called *opus sectile*. The destruction of this gem of early Christian architecture is recorded by Ugonio in the following words: "This most splendid oratory was torn down amid the groans of the City, and its destruction has left a sense of loss in the hearts of all."

The closing years of the sixteenth century fall in the pontificate of Pope Clement VIII., Aldobrandini (1592–1605). He undertook, in 1597, the renovation of the transept of St. John Lateran, which was called, after him, the Nave Clementina. He also raised the magnificent Altar of the Sacrament at the south end of the same transept. The names of Pietro Paolo Olivieri, architect; of Cav. di Arpino and Cristoforo dalle Pomarancie, painters; of Antonio Valsoldo, Francesco Landini, and Silla Longhi, sculptors; of Curzio Vanni, goldsmith; of Orazio Censori, founder; and of Giulio Lanciani, goldbeater, are associated with this important work. But what a destruction of old marbles and bronzes the completion of it involved! It is clear from the account-book of the clerk of the works, Giovanni Vaccarone, that for three consecutive years Rome, the suburbs, and even parts of Etruria were ransacked to secure materials. Damages were caused not so much by the small private speculators who provided, one a column, another a bit of frieze, or a tombstone, or plain blocks of marble, as by the contractors armed with the Pope's official permission to carry off or pull to pieces any antique monument that would suit their purpose.

Among those mentioned as having provided materials — those who destroyed old monuments on their own account — are Muzio del Bufalo; Flaminio Vacca, who sold the marbles of the arch of Claudius in the Piazza di Sciarra; the nuns of S. Silvestro, who furnished marbles from the temple of Mithras at S. Giovannino (Via della Mercede); Loreto Facciolo, who thus disposed of the remains of the temple of Venus in Calcararo; the canons of the Pantheon, who sold the marbles from the Baths of Agrippa; the monks of La Minerva, who apparently furnished marbles from the temple of Isis; the nuns of S. Marta, who sold the remains of the Arco di Camigliano; and the Duchess Savelli, who sold I know not what splendid remains. The monks of SS. Apostoli contributed a column of porphyry and a block of giallo antico; the nuns of S. Lorenzo in Panisperna, many blocks of travertine from some ruins which occupied the slope of the Viminal, in the neighbourhood of S. Pudenziana; the priests of S. Agnese, in the Piazza Navona, furnished stone and marble from the Alexandrine Stadium; and there were a hundred others that I cannot take the space to mention.

Meanwhile the papal board of works on its own account undertook excavations and the demolition of ruins, granting two-thirds of the proceeds to those who did the work. Under these conditions Alessandro Senzolino carried on systematic operations in the Forum and at La Marmorata; Petruccio Bettania, at Ostia; Gioacchino Borrella, at Ponte Salario; Ottaviano da Gubbio, at the Torre Pignattara and S. Maria Nuova, that is, the mausoleum of the Empress Helena and the temple of Venus and Rome. They took columns wherever they could find them, not only from sacred edifices, like the old Lateran, S. Croce in Gerusalemme, and S. Pudenziana, but even from the street corners. On April 25, 1599, a Pietro Savia, a mason, sold "the shaft of a column of giallo taken from the corner of a house near S. Apollinare." On the same day a certain Ippolito conveyed a similar shaft "removed from the corner of his vineyard at the Sette Sale," and on May 2, Simon the apothecary sold a piece of portasanta, which had served as a curbstone at the entrance to the Ponte Sisto.

The worst deeds of destruction at this time, however, must be brought home to Orazio Censori, the builder of the Altar of the Sacrament. This masterpiece is ornamented with four large bronze-gilt columns, which support a pediment of the same metal. The guide-books relate fantastic stories as to the origin of these four columns. One account assigns them to the temple of Jupiter Optimus Maximus; according to another, the Emperor Vespasian brought them from Judaea; and a third version says that they were cast by Augustus from the beaks of the ships captured at the battle of Actium. It is probably true that the columns, or at least two of them, were placed in the Lateran by Constantine, to serve as light-bearers (*Pharo-cantharoi*) on each side of the high altar.

As the necessary metal was lacking to adapt the columns to the design of the new altar, and to crown them with capitals and a pediment, Censori made a tour in Etruria, in the district of Tarquinii and Falerii. He brought back to Rome hundreds upon hundreds of pounds of works of art in bronze, collected from the tombs of Corneto and Civita Castellana, which were all melted up in the furnace, together with pieces of the bronze beams of the Pantheon. An entry dated July, 1599, records the payment of 5089.55 scudi to Censori "for mending a broken bronze column; for the manufacture of three new capitals with foliage, flowers, rosettes, and ovules; for the decorations of the entire cornice, consisting of 16 doves, 16 stars, and 2 large angels; and for the expenses of his journey to Corneto and Civita Castellana, to bring metal to Rome." The commune of Corneto received 59.85 scudi for 66) pounds of bronze; I have not found the account relative to Città Castellana.

In opposition to this shameful behaviour of the Apostolic chamber, the City Council never granted

Fig. 43.—The Loggia of Pietro Squarcialupi, Palazzo del Senatore.

permission to use materials from ancient structures without restrictions designed to protect the structures themselves. On September, 1520, Pietro Squarcialupi, Senator, wishing to complete the Loggia in front of the Palazzo del Senatore on the Capitol (Fig. 43), asked permission to obtain stones from the neighbourhood of the triumphal arch of Septimius Severus. The decree of the Council granting the authorisation is a model of

FIG. 44. — The Ponte Rotto, half carried away by the inundation of 1557.

prudence. The Senator must excavate on his own responsibility and at his own expense; and when the excavation has reached the desired depth he must notify the magistrate, who, with a committee of ten citizens, "shall visit the place, and satisfy himself that no harm is done to the standing remains of the arch, or of other monuments in the Forum."

A similar instance may be quoted from the Records of the latter half of the century. On October 15, 1574, the City Council, pressed by Pope Gregory XIII. to restore the Ponte Rotto (the Pons Aemilius of classic times, Fig. 44), three arches of which had been carried away by the inundation of September 27, 1557, accepted the suggestion of Giovanni Battista Cecchini, the chairman of the Council, to make use of blocks of travertine from the Coliseum for the work. The decree of the Council, however, was worded with the greatest care: "It is agreed that the marbles and stones required for the work shall be excavated and removed from the belt of ruins around the amphitheatre, commonly called il Coliseo, provided that the said marbles and stones are found loose, and in no way attached to any standing part of the monument. The search can be extended to other sites belonging to the S. P. Q. R.,[1] provided no harm is done to standing ruins — Matteo da Castello, our architect, to carry out the instructions

[1] *Senatus Populusque Romanus*, "The Senate and People of Rome," an official designation of the government of the modern as well as of the ancient city.

of the Council; all statues, or movable antiquities, which may eventually come to light, shall be the property of the S. P. Q. R."

In this connexion it is worth while to remark that the founders of the science of epigraphy, Metello, Smetius, Pighius, Ligorio, Panvinio, Fulvio Ursino, and Cittadini, aimed simply to copy the greatest possible number of inscriptions, and to investigate and expound their meaning; they concerned themselves not at all with such matters as the place in which an inscription was discovered, or its subsequent fate. They did not seem to think it important to notice whether a block containing an inscription had been found in situ, or loose in a mass of rubbish, whether in the Forum or in the Campus Martius. Once an inscription was copied and made known, it was a matter of indifference to them whether the original stone was removed to the Farnese, Cesi, or Carpi museums, or burnt into lime, or sawed into slabs to pave the floor of St. Peter's. A full recognition of the importance of recording the minutest details in all branches of study having to do with antiquity has come only with the development of scientific method in our own days.

CHAPTER XX

THE MODERNISATION OF MEDIAEVAL BUILDINGS IN THE SEVENTEENTH AND EIGHTEENTH CENTURIES

THE systematic demolition of the remains of ancient Rome ends with the sixteenth century, but the next period, which extends from the beginning of the seventeenth to the end of the eighteenth century, adds another chapter to the record of loss and disappearance — the destruction of mediaeval buildings. Under the pretext of restoration and embellishment, popes, cardinals, patricians, and heads of monastic orders, laid their hands upon the most noted and the most venerable churches, which had, until then, preserved their beautiful basilica type in all its simplicity and majesty. Paul V., as we have seen, inaugurated the movement by pulling down the east half of the old basilica of St. Peter's, 1606-1615. The seventeenth century witnessed, also, other modernisations; the twin churches of St. Hadrian and S. Martina were disfigured by Piero da Cortona, under Urban VIII., and by Alfonzo Sotomayor and Borromini, under Alexander VII. In 1651, Onorio Longhi destroyed the church of S. Ambrogio with its marvellous frescoes by Pierino del Vaga, to build in its place the tasteless structure of S. Carlo al Corso.

In the eighteenth century the list is rapidly extended. The old church of S. Alessio was modernised by Tommaso de Marchis in 1750, the church of S. Anastasia, in 1722, by Carlo Gimach. The disfigurement of S. Apollinare was due to Ferdinando Fuga, of SS. Apostoli to Francesco Fontana, and of SS. Cosma e Damiano to Arrigucci. The basilica of S. Croce in Gerusalemme was profaned and reduced to its present form in 1744 by Passalacqua and Gregorini, a restoration classed by Milizia among the works of "nefarious" architects. The same title of dishonour was given by Fea to Paolo Posi, who, under Benedict XIV., profaned the attic of the Pantheon, substituting chiaroscuro daubs for the exquisite marble incrustations of the time of Septimius Severus. The epithet "nefarious," might most appropriately be applied also to Borromini on account of the disfigurement of the Lateran, to Antonio Canevari for that of SS. Giovanni e Paolo, to Francesco Ferrari for that of S. Gregorio on the Caelian, and so on to wearisome length; for the restoration of churches became a general practice, and was carried out in accordance with a uniform plan.

This plan may be easily outlined. "The columns of the nave were walled up, and concealed in thick pilasters of whitewashed masonry; the inscribed, or sculptured marble slabs, and the cosmatesque pavements, were taken up and replaced by brick floors; the windows were enlarged out of all proportion, that floods of light might enter and illuminate every remote, peaceful recess of the sacred edifice. For the beautiful roofs made of cedar wood, vaults or lacunaria were substituted. The simple but precious frescoes of the fourteenth century were whitewashed, and the fresh surface was covered with the insignificant productions of Francesco Cozza, Gerolamo Troppa, Giacinto Brandi, and other painters equally obscure."[1] But the most surprising fact is that all these profanations could be accomplished, not only without opposition, but amid general applause; such was the perverted taste of the time.

In this period, however, we are called upon to chronicle only a few instances of the destruction of classical monuments. Paul V., in 1610, demolished the Baths of Constantine and four churches to make room for the palace of his kinsman, Scipione Borghese, now the Rospigliosi palace. He also levelled to the ground the beautiful remains of the temple of Minerva in the Forum Transitorium (1606); the columns and frieze were cut into slabs and utilised for the decoration of the Borghese Chapel in S. Maria Maggiore, and of the fountain of the Acqua Paola on the Janiculum. The blocks of stone belonging to the cella of the temple,

[1] *Ancient Rome*, p. xix.

and to the enclosing wall of the Forum were given to the monks of S. Adriano.

In 1632 Urban VIII. damaged the Templum Sacrae Urbis and the Heroon Romuli, which are united in the church of SS. Cosma e Damiano. He raised the level of both buildings twenty-four feet, and sold or presented stones from them to the Jesuits for their church of S. Ignazio. The bronze doors were wrenched from their fastenings and reset out of place; the historic inscriptions were obliterated, and the beautiful veneering of marble in *opus sectile* was destroyed. Urban is responsible also for the destruction of the Secretarium Senatus (S. Martina), of some portions of the mausoleum of Hadrian, of the old churches of S. Vibiana, S. Anastasia, S. Maria in Pallara, and S. Salvatore in Campo, and lastly of the bronze roof which covered the portico of the Pantheon. The weight of the metal removed to the apostolic foundry from the Pantheon was 450,251 pounds.

The last incident we have to mention in this connexion is the demolition of the triumphal arch which stood at the corner of the Corso (Via Flaminia) and the Via in Lucina (Ara Pacis), accomplished by Pope Alexander VII. in 1662. Two of the bas-reliefs were removed to the Capitoline Museum; a third was given to Maria Peretti Savelli. Two columns of verde antico were bought by the Pamphili and placed on either side of their altar at S. Agnese in the Piazza Navona; two others found a resting-place in the Corsini Chapel at the Lateran. The key of the arch is to be found in the vestibule of the University of Rome, and the group of the three dancing Hours, discovered in 1740 at the foot of the arch, has been removed to the Galleria delle Statue in the Vatican Museum.

CHAPTER XXI

MODERN USE OF ANCIENT MARBLES

IF we could only wrest the secret of their origin from the marbles, stones, and bricks with which our palaces, our houses, and our churches were built and decorated in the period of the Renaissance, if the marble-dust with which the ceilings and the walls were plastered, and their stucco ornamentation modelled, by the cinquecento artists, could be again moulded into the statues and bas-reliefs from which it was obtained, our knowledge of the ancient City and of its treasures of art would be wonderfully enhanced. We cannot follow the record of this practice without a feeling of melancholy as we reflect upon the irreparable loss to culture and progress which the modern world has experienced in the disappearance of so many masterpieces in which were embodied the highest ideals of antiquity. Nothing would better illustrate the strange turns of fortune than the varied uses to which the marbles from ancient structures have been put in modern times; and I may, perhaps, fittingly close this brief sketch by relating a few out of the almost numberless instances that have come to my notice.

The beautiful slabs of portasanta, with which the doors of the church of S. Maria dell' Anima are veneered, were taken from a marble-cutter's shop, discovered in the foundations of the same church. The tombstone of Inigo Piccolomini, Duke of Amalfi, Marquis of Capistrano, Chief Justice of the kingdom of Naples, buried August 29, 1566, in S. Maria del Popolo, was cut out of a cornice from the Baths of Agrippa.

We know from the Memoirs of Flaminio Vacca that the coat of arms of Pius IV. on the Porta Pia was carved out of the capital of a column of the Porticus Eventus Boni near the Stagnum Agrippae.[1] In the same connexion Vacca says: " I remember also that while the Theatine Fathers were laying the foundations of the church of S. Andrea della Valle they found a part of a column of grey granite forty palms long. This was sawn into several pieces, and one of them was turned into the threshold of the main door of the church."

Vacca further throws light on the disappearance of the last remains of the temple of Jupiter Optimus Maximus. "Upon the Tarpeian rock behind the Palazzo dei Conservatori," he says, "several columns of Pentelic marble were found. Their capitals were so large that I was able to carve out of one the lion which is now in the loggia of the Villa Medici facing the garden. The others were used by Vincenzo de Rossi for the statues of the prophets and other figures

[1] See p. 3.

which adorn the chapel of Cardinal Cesi in the church of S. Maria della Pace (Fig. 45). No fragment of the

FIG. 45.— The Cesi chapel in the church of S. Maria della Pace, built with Pentelic marble from the temple of Jupiter Optimus Maximus.

entablature was found, but as the building was close to the edge of the Tarpeian rock I suspect that its marbles must have fallen over the precipice " (Mem. 64).

The correctness of this surmise was proved in 1780, one hundred and eighty years after the publication of Vacca's Memoirs. "In that year," says Montagnani, "great blocks of entablature of beautiful workmanship were found under the house at No. 13 Via Montanara, belonging to Duke Lante della Rovere. The frieze was ornamented with festoons fastened to the heads of bulls. They were destroyed on the spot before any one could make a sketch of them. As this house of Duke Lante stands at the foot of the Capitoline hill, I have no doubt that the marbles belong to the temple mentioned by Vacca."

Toward the middle of the fifteenth century a number of fluted columns of giallo antico thirteen feet long were discovered among the ruins of the temple of Venus in the gardens of Sallust. Cardinal Ricci di Montepulciano bought them and used them for the balustrade in his chapel in S. Pietro in Montorio. He purchased also some alabaster columns found at the same place, which he had sawed into slabs for tables; these and other valuable objects were shipped to Lisbon as a present to the King of Portugal, but the vessel which bore them foundered in a gale.

When the tepidarium or central hall of the Baths of Diocletian was adapted for Christian worship by Pius IV. the capital of one of the eight granite pillars was missing; Michel Angelo replaced it by another discovered accidentally among the ruins of the temple of Claudius on the

Caelian. The stadium of Domitian, now represented by the Piazza Navona, has supplied materials for the erection of several modern buildings, among them the palace of Beneinbene in the Piazza Madama, the church of S. Nicola dei Lorenesi in the Via dell' Anima, and the Casino of Pius IV. in the Vatican gardens.

The chapel of Gregory XIII. in St. Peter's is mostly built with marbles from the mausoleum of Hadrian. Giovanni Alberti, who happened to be in Rome at the time of its erection, has left the following memorandum in his sketch-book, now in the Collacchioni library, Borgo S. Sepolcro: "The frieze with wreaths and bulls' heads, sketched on these sheets, together with the architrave and base, was taken from the river-front of the mausoleum of Hadrian by order of Pope Gregory XIII. The marbles will be used in building the Gregorian Chapel in St. Peter's. I made these drawings July 20, 1579." A similar fate befell the marbles discovered in the Augusteum of the Fratres Arvales, near La Magliana. The Augusteum was an oblong hall, supported by columns of Greek marble twenty-two feet high. It contained statues of imperial members of the brotherhood, standing on pedestals inscribed with their praises. The statues were saved and were dispersed among several collections; the columns and pedestals were cut up for the decoration of the same chapel.

Up to about the middle of the sixteenth century there were considerable remains of the Baths of Titus standing east of the Coliseum, between S. Pietro in Vincoli and the Baths of Trajan.[1] Here were found sections of "the most beautiful cornices," which, according to the prevailing custom, were sawed up into slabs, and were sold to the Jesuits to be used in their church of Gesù. The mention of this church brings to my memory another incident of the same sort. From the beautiful volume lately published by Plon in Paris,[2] we learn that in or about 1541, the head of the Roman house of the Jesuits, Father Condatius, unearthed in the piazza then called degli Altieri, now del Gesù, some great blocks of marble which he sold for one hundred ducats. Another document which I have discovered in the state archives tells us that the marbles were bought by a lime-burner and consumed in a kiln close to the church.

The columns of verde antico which ornament the balcony of the Farnese palace, and those of the villa of Julius III. on the Via Flaminia, come from the Baths of the Acque Albule, or sulphur springs, in the plain below Tivoli. The columns of rare breccia on the high altar of the church of S. Rocco are from an ancient building on the site of the present Orto Botanico. The two alabaster columns of the Odescalchi Chapel in the SS. Apostoli were found in 1728 in the palace of Au-

[1] They are represented on sheets 17 and 18 of the *Vestigi dell' antichità di Roma* of du Perac (edition of 1575).

[2] *La vie de Saint Ignace de Loyola d'après Pierre Ribadeneira, son premier historien*, par le P. Charles Clair, S.J., p. 278.

gustus on the Palatine. The vestibule of the church of S. Teodoro is paved with pieces of porphyry found at La Marmorata. The uppermost steps of the Porto di Ripetta, removed in 1888, were paved with blocks of serpentine from the same place. The piazza and the inclined approach of the Capitol were paved with travertine slabs from the area in front of the Pantheon. The columns of breccia corallina in the chapel of S. Sebastiano on the Palatine come from the house of the Vestals; those of the chapel of the Morti in S. Lorenzo fuori le Mura from the police barracks on the Caelian (castra Peregrinorum).

The Ginetti chapel in S. Andrea della Valle is inlaid with slabs of Africano discovered at Porto; the Falconieri Chapel in S. Giovanni dei Fiorentini, with marbles from the great temple of Juno at Veii; the Borghese Chapel in S. Maria Maggiore, with the spoils of the temples and palaces on the Aventine; and the Bernini palace at S. Andrea delle Fratte, modernised by the present owner in 1868, with the spoils of the Baths of Licinius Sura. The terminal tower of the city wall on the left bank of the Tiber below Monte Testaccio was built by Honorius or Narses with blocks of alabaster from the neighbouring marble-wharf; at the beginning of the last century the tower was pulled down and the blocks were used again for the chapel of Raphael in the Pantheon.

When we think of the wealth of marbles displayed

in the public and private buildings of Rome, and at the same time consider that every cubic foot has been obtained from the monuments of the ancient City, we gain a new insight into the magnitude of the building operations of the ancient Romans. We must remember, too, that the greater part of the ancient marbles used by modern architects and marble-workers were found either shapeless or in a form unsuited to the use for which they were needed, so that at least from a third to a half of the gross cubic content has been lost.

In 1845 Faustino Corsi made a list of the marble columns dispersed over the fourteen wards of the city; the total number recorded by him is 7012. Since the publication of this catalogue fifty-four years have elapsed, and we may calculate that the number has been increased by at least one-tenth, so that to-day the sum total is probably not far from 8000. This is truly a surprising number, but it is far from incredible, if we recall that the City once possessed 3000 statues of bronze alone.

INDEXES

I. INDEX OF SUBJECTS

ABBEY, Westminster, 184, 187 fol.
Acqua Paola, fountain of, 255.
Acque Albule, baths of, 263.
Adalbert, Count, gives warning of the approach of the Saracens, 127.
S. Adriano. See Church, under Hadrian.
Aesculapius, statue of, 29.
St. Agatha, *posterula* of, 139 fol.; church of, 145, 147.
Agilulf, 88.
S. Agnese fuori le Mura, garden of, 20; church of, 20, 32.
S. Agnese (Piazza Navona), church of, 246, 256.
S. Agostino, church of, 204.
Agrippa, improvement of Rome, 11; Pantheon of, 110; statue of, 111; head of (?), 112.
Agrippae Stagnum, 259.
Aix-la-Chapelle, cathedral of, 183.
Alaric, 53, 91, 115; advance on Rome in 408, 56; enters the city in 410, 57.
Albinus, Lucius, 112.
Aldobrandini gardens, 24.
S. Alessio, church of, 254.
Alexander VI., VII. See Pope.
Altar of the Sacrament, bronze columns of, 247.
S. Ambrogio, church of, 253.
Anastasis (S. Anastasia). See Church.
S. Andrea at Amalfi, church of, 184; delle Frate, 264; at the Manger, 118; della Valle, 4, 259, 264.
SS. Andreae et Gregorii ad Clivum Scaurum, church, 121.
S. Angelo, castle of, 8, 88, 128, 133, 156, 160, 177, 214.

Anguillara, 199.
Anicii, 199.
Anicius Acilius Aginatius, 37; Paulinus, 36.
Annia Cornificia Faustina, house of, 57.
Annibaldi, 201.
S. Anselmo, garden of, 57.
Antiochia, statue of, 104.
Antonio da Sangallo, the younger, memorandum of, 32.
Antonius and Faustina, temple of, 111.
S. Apollinare, church of, 246, 254.
Apollo Belvedere, 222.
SS. Apostoli. See Church.
Apoxyomenos, copy of, 69.
Appian Way. See Via Appia.
Apusii, tomb of the, 103.
Aqua Alexandrina, 240; Anio Vetus, 82; Appia, 82; Claudia, 80, 85, 240; Felice, 82, 85, 240, 242; Marcia, 80, 85, 240; Virgo, 82.
Aqueducts, water supply of, cut off by Goths, 79; channels of, neglected, 80 fol.; used for fortifications, 83. Also, see Aqua.
Ara Maxima, 17, 209.
Aracoeli, church of the, 220.
Arcadius, inscription relating to, 50; restored city walls, 53; with Honorius repaired theatre of Pompey, 152.
Arcadius, Honorius, and Theodosius. See Arch.
Arch, of Arcadius, Honorius, and Theodosius, 52, 53, 151; of M. Aurelius, on the Corso, 118, 231, 256 fol.; di Camigliano, 245; of Claudius, 148,

267

245; of Constantine, 19, 30, 201; of Gratianus, Valentinianus, and Theodosius, 52, 151, 207; of Gordianus, 211; of Janus Quadrifrons (of the Forum Boarium), 34, 125, 201, 235, 241; of Lentulus, 191; *arcus novus* (near S. Maria in Via Lata), 210; of Septimius Severus, 145, 147, 148, 251; of Titus, 121, 151, 201; of Trajan, 31; of Valentinian and Valens, 53.

Architectus publicorum, 77.

Arcus Caelimontani, 78.

Argiletum, 147, 153.

Ariadne, statue of the sleeping, 222.

Ariulf, 88.

Arruntii, tomb of the, 31.

Art(orius?) Germanianus, house of, 24.

Augusteum, 110; of the Fratres Arvales, 262.

Augustus, transformation of the city during the administration of, 10 fol.; places images of the gods in the Compital shrines, 38; statue of, 111; mausoleum of, 170, 176, 199; palace of, on the Palatine, 263 fol.

Aurelian, walls of, 15.

Aurelius, Marcus, 58; column of, 109, 125, 166, 238, 239; bronze equestrian statue of, 222, 231 fol. See Arch.

Aurelius Avianius Symmachus, L., house of, 45, 77.

Aventine, finds on the, 61 fol.

Avidius Quietus, house of, 24.

Avignon, seat of papacy at, 198.

Bacchus, statue of the Indian, 29.

Baccio Pontelli, buildings erected by, 204.

S. Balbina, church of, 198.

Balbus, L. Cornelius, 11; capacity of theatre of, 5; cryptus of, 157, 176, 177.

Barbarians not accountable for the disappearance of Roman monuments, 7.

Bartoli, extracts from the memoirs of Pietro Santo, 40, 62, 90.

Basilica of Junius Bassus, 118; of Constantine, 110; Eudoxiana, 75; Jovis, 177; Julia, 22, 36, 91, 157, 191, 194, 211; Salvatoris in Laterano, 33. See Church.

Bathing establishment discovered on the Esquiline, 28.

Baths, of the Acque Albule, 263; of the Julii Akarii, 152; of Licinius Sura, 204; of Livia on the Palatine, 23. See Thermae.

Bath-tubs, pagan, used for holding the relics of martyrs, 117.

Belisarius, 75, 79.

Belvedere, 204; torso of, 222.

Benedict V., VI., VIII., IX., XIV. See Pope.

Bernini, Lorenzo, discovery made by, 41.

Boniface IV., VI., VIII. See Pope.

Borgia. See Pope.

Bove, Capo di, 236. See Caecilia Metella.

Bramante, buildings erected by, 204; designs for St. Peter's, 212.

Bridge, Aemilian (Pons Aemilius, Ponte Rotto), 199, 232, 251; of S. Angelo (Aelian), 41, 142 fol., 177, 178; of Cestius (S. Bartolomeo), 34; Milvian, 208; of Valentinian (Ponte Sisto), 34, 246; Vatican (Pons Vaticanus *or* Neronianus), 53, 151, 208.

Burgus, the quarter, 128; walls of, 132 fol., 136, 177.

Burial-places. See Tombs.

Byzantine colony about the Palatine, 122.

S. Caecilia, church of, 116.

Caecilia Metella, tomb of, 92, 96, 191, 236 fol.

Caelestinus II. See Pope.

Caelian, market hall on (S. Stefano Rotondo), 34, 37; suffered from Norman-Saracenic invasion, 162.

Caesar, Julius, statue of, 232; statue of a young, 104.

Caetani, the, 201.

Calcararii, 180 fol.; headquarters of, 193.

Cameos. See Gems.

INDEX OF SUBJECTS

Campagna, 153; outlaws of, 158; final desolation of, 101.
Campo di Fiori, 5.
Canale di Fiumicino, 33.
Capitolium, 12, 143, 145, 153, 189, 248, 264. See Museum.
Caracalla, 22. See Thermae.
Carinae, 201.
S. Carlo al Corso, church of, 254.
Cartularia, Turris, 121, 201.
Caryatides of Diogenes, 111.
Casal Rotondo, 237.
Casino dei Quattro Venti, 16.
Cassino, Monte, cathedral of, 184 fol.
Cassiodorius, 38, 77 fol., 183.
Castor and Pollux, statues of, 232 fol.
Catacombs, abandoned after the Gothic invasion, 70, 91; devasted by the barbarians, 70 fol.; who encamped about the entrance to, 71; restorations of, 71; relics of martyrs transferred from, 106, 115 fol.
Cathedrals, partially built of Roman marbles; Aix-la-Chapelle, 183; Pisa, and others, 184 fol.; Westminster Abbey, 187 fol.
Celer, Nero's architect, 19; his mausoleum and epitaph, 20.
Celestine IV. See Pope.
S. Celso in Banchi, church of, 151, 208.
SS. Celso and Giuliano, church of, 213.
Cemeteries, ancient, covered over, 15, 16; cameos and gems found on the sites of Christian, 94 fol.
S. Cesario in Palatio, church of, 106, 120; monasterium of, 120.
Cespian hill, 40.
Cestius, Gaius, tomb of, 96, 178.
Cestius (S. Bartolomeo), bridge of, 34.
Christopher. See Pope.
Church, of S. Agatha, 145, 147; S. Agnese, 20, 32 (Piazza Navona), 246, 256; S. Agostino, 204; S. Alessio, 254; S. Ambrogio, 253; S. Anastasia (Anastasis, the Resurrection), 122, 175, 176, 254, 256; S. Andrea ad Amalfi, 184; S. Andrea della Frate, 264; St. Andrew at the Manger, 118; S. Andrea della Valle, 4, 259, 264; SS. Andreae et Gregorii ad Clivum Scaurum, 121; S. Apollinare, 246, 254; SS. Apostoli, 116, 204, 245, 254, 263; of the Aracoeli, 220; S. Balbina, 198; S. Caecilia, 116; S. Carlo al Corso, 254; S. Celso in Banchi, 151, 208; SS. Celso e Giuliano, 213; S. Cesario in Palatio, 106, 120; S. Ciriaco (S. Cyriacus), 91, 137, 147; S. Clemente, 33, 162; SS. Cosma e Damiano, 37, 110, 118 (Subiaco), 137, 254, 256; S. Croce in Gerusalemme, 246, 254; S. Dionysius, 110, 139; S. Donatus, 213; S. Euplos, 122; S. Euphemia in Vico Patricii, 145, 148; S. Eustachio, 191; S. Francesca Romana, 175; Gesù, 263; S. Galla Patricia, 177; S. Giacomo del Colosseo, 89; S. Giacomo Scossa-Cavalli, 178; S. Giorgio in Velabro, 122, 125, 241; S. Giovanni dei Fiorentini, 264; (see St. John); S. Giovanni e Paolo, 254; S. Girolamo degli Schiavoni, 239; S. Gregorio, 254; St. Hadrian (S. Adriano), 110, 123, 145, 147, 165, 175, 253, 256; S. Ignazio, 256; St. John Lateran, 123, 159, 206, 207, 234, 239, 244, 246, 251 (see Lateran); St. Lawrence, 110; S. Laurentius in Porticu Maiore, 178; of the Ordo, 178; S. Laurentius in Damaso, 145; S. Laurentius in Pensilis, 147; S. Laurentius in Formoso, 145, 148; S. Laurentius in Prasino, 145, 146; S. Lorenzo fuori le Mura (St. Lawrence on the Via Tiburtina), 33, 40, 132, 136, 264; S. Lorenzo in Panisperna, 246; S. Lucia de Calcarario (S. Lucia dei Ginnasi), 193; S. Lucia in Selce, 142, 147; S. Marcello, 90; Marcelli, 213; S. Maria dell' Anima, 259; S. Maria Antiqua, 110; S. Maria in Campitelli, 91; S. Maria in Cosmedin, 34, 176, 208; S. Maria delle Grazie, 91; S. Maria Liberatrice, 120; S. Maria Maggiore, 175, 204, 239, 241, 255, 264; S. Maria ad Martyres (Pantheon), 90, 110 fol., 115; S. Maria in Monticelli, 165; S. Maria Nova, 103; S. Maria Nuova, 91, 175, 246; S. Maria della Pace,

INDEX OF SUBJECTS

204, 260; S. Maria in Pallara, 256; S. Maria del Popolo, 204, 259; S. Maria in Schola Greca, 122; S. Maria del Sole, 12; S. Maria Transpontina, 178; S. Maria in Trastevere, 152; S. Maria in Via Lata, 139, 210; S. Maria in Virgari, 178; S. Martina, 110, 118, 231, 253; S. Martino ai Monti, 79; S. Michele in Borgo, 117; La Minerva, 171, 205, 245; St. Nicholas, 169; St. Nicolaus in Calcaria (S. Nicolo ai Cesarini), 193; S. Nicolo in Calcarario, 90; S. Nicolo dei Lorenesi, 262; S. Orso, 151; St. Pancras, 79, 243; S. Pantaleo ai Monti, 165; (see Pantheon = Rotonda;) St. Paul's without the walls (S. Paolo fuori le Mura), 33, 60, 117, 128, 132, 135 fol., 143, 181; St. Peter's, 8, 52, 60, 72, 117, 122, 128, 151, 175, 177, 178, 191, 208, 212, 213, 217, 219, 253, 262; S. Phocas, 122; S. Pietro in Montorio, 190, 204, 261; S. Pietro in Vincoli, 75, 148, 204; S. Prisca, 61; S. Praesede, 116; S. Pudens in Vico Patricio, 145, 148 ; S. Pudenziana, 246: SS. Quaranta de Calcarario (S. Francesco delle Stimmate), 193; SS. Quatro Coronati, 165, 181; SS. Quirico e Giolitta, 147 ; S. Rocco, 263; S. Saba, 122; S. Sabina, 61; S. Salvatore in Campo, 256; S. Salvator de Porticu, 178; S. Salvatore in Primicerio, 165; of the Saviour, 110 ; S. Sebastiano in Pallara, 91 ; S. Sebastiano alla Polveriera, 121; SS. Sergius et Bacchus, 110, 145, 146; S. Silvestro in Capite (St. Sylvester), 139, 166, 219, 245 ; Sistine Chapel, 204 ; S. Stefano delle Carozze, 12 ; S. Stefano Rotondo, 34, 37 ; S. Susanna, 242; S. Teodoro, 117, 122, 264; S. Vibiana, 116, 256; S. Vitalis in Vico Longo, 145, 148, 192.

Churches outside the walls abandoned, 126. See Cathedrals.

Circus Maximus, 4, 17, 19, 48, 66, 143, 151, 170, 176, 191, 207; Flaminius, 66, 145, 146, 147, 157, 193; of Nero, 32.

S. Ciriaco (S. Cyriacus). See Church.

Città Castellana, 13, 247.
Civitas Leonina. See Burgus.
Claudia Vera, house of, 24.
Claudius (Caelian), temple of, 208, 261; bust of, 196.
Claudius Claudianus, house of, 24.
Clement VII, VIII. See Pope.
S. Clemente, church of, 33, 162.
Clergy, ignorance of the Roman, 117.
Clivus Argentarius, 147 ; Capitolinus, 34; Sacer, 22, 36; Scauri, 19; Suburanus, 63, 147; Victoriae, 120.
Clodius Hermogenianus, 36.
Coliseum (Flavian Amphitheatre), 28, 34, 48, 77, 89, 125, 175, 191, 201, 206, 207, 208, 211, 251.
Collegium Fortunae Felicis, offices of, 27.
Colonna family, 199.
Comes formarum urbis, 78.
Comes portus urbis Romae, 78.
Commodus, bust of, 222.
Compital shrines, adorned by Augustus, 38.
Concord, temple of, 110, 206.
Conflagrations, described by Livy, 16; under the Emperor Nero, in 64 A.D., 17 fol.; traces of this fire, 19; in the Forum Romanum, 21 fol.; in the reign of Titus, 80 A.D., 22, 28; in the reign of Commodus, 191 A.D., 22; in the reign of Carinus in 283 A.D., 22; in 1084 A.D., 160 fol.
Constans II., visit to Rome in 663 A.D., 8, 92, 111, 123 fol.
Constantia, mausoleum of, 32.
Constantine, 29; dismantled earlier buildings, 31 ; and erected the basilica of St. Peter's, 31 fol.; regionary catalogue compiled in the time of, 48; equestrian statues of, 145, 153; statues of, 222. See Arch, Basilica, Thermae.
Constantius II., 34, 47 fol.
Corneto, treasures from, 247.
Cornificius, Lucius, 11.
Corridojo di Castello, 133.
Cortile di Belvedere, 90.
Cortina beati Petri, 178.
SS. Cosma e Damiano. See Church.

INDEX OF SUBJECTS

Cosmatis, school of, 34, 180 fol., 203.
Cosmus, house of, 58.
Craticulae Templum, 177.
Crescenzi, the, 200.
S. Croce in Gerusalemme, church of, 246, 254.
Curator Statuarum, 34.
Curia. See Senate-house.
Cybele, statue of, 70, 112.
Cypress, the, 145 fol.

S. Damaso, court of, 204.
Damasus. See Pope.
Dea Dia, temple of, 208.
Decii. See Thermae.
Decius Albinus, Caecina, 61; Marius Venantius Basilius, 77; Trajanus, 28.
"Destruction" and "Disappearance" of Roman monuments, distinction in meaning, 4.
Destruction of Roman villas, causes of, 101; of monuments in Roman and in modern times, 189 fol.
Destruction of Rome, three facts prominent in the history of, 13 fol.
Diocletian, 29; repairs buildings in the Forum, 22; triumph of, 49 fol.; statue of, 104. See Thermae.
St. Dionysius, church of, 110, 139.
Domitian, house of, on the Palatine, 119; villa of, 186.
Domus Gaiana, 120; Pinciana, 38, 183.
St. Donatus, church of, 213.

Elephantus Herbarius, 176.
Ephebus, statuette of, 196.
Equestrian group, pedestal of, found in Forum, 50.
Esquiline hill, covered over and raised by Augustus, 14; the event commemorated by Horace, 15; marketplace on, 34; gate of, 147.
Eugenius, defeat of, 35.
Eugenius IV. See Pope.
S. Euphemia in Vico Patricii, church of, 145, 148.
S. Euplos, church of, 122.
S. Eustachio, church of, 191.
Euterpe, statue of, 104.

Eventus Bonus, colonnade of, 4.
Excavations, in the time of Pope Eugenius IV., 112; of Sixtus IV., 66; of Innocent VIII., 103; of Pius IV., 5, 61; in 1724 (Palatine), 119; in 1762 (Villa Quintiliorum), 103; in 1780 (Appian Way), 105; in time of Pope Pius VI., 104; by Carlo Torlonia, 104; in 1849, 69; in 1855, 105; in 1862, 5; in 1864, 66; in 1867-68 (at Ostia), 127; in 1869 (Palatine), 119, 196, (Via Severiana), 93; in 1873 (Esquiline), 28; in 1875 (Esquiline), 94; in 1876, 5; in 1877 (near the Coliseum), 19, (Via Nazionale), 23; in 1879 (Thermae of Constantine), 24; in 1880 (Site of the English Church), 69; in 1883 (House of the Vestals), 121, 196; by Boccanera in 1883-84, 105; in 1885 (Teatro Drammatico), 66; in 1886, 13, (Piazza Bocca della Verità), 17, (Esquiline), 42; in 1887, 14; in 1888 (Temple of Isis), 42; in 1891, 4; in 1892 (garden of S. Sabina), 58; in 1895 (near the Coliseum), 89; in 1896 (Piazza Bocca della Verità), 39; in the Vigna Torlonia and Vigna Maciocchi, 57.

Fabbrica di S. Pietro, 228, 235.
Fabii, tomb of the, 31.
Fabius Felix Passifilus Paulinus, 36; Titianus, 36.
Factionis Prasinae Stabula, 146.
Falerii, 13.
Fates, group of the Three, 87.
Ficoroni, Francesco di, 41, 91 fol.
Flavinus Philippus, 151.
Fontana, Domenico (architect of Sixtus V.), 85, 238, 240, 241.
Formosus. See Pope.
Forum of Augustus, 112.
Forum Boarium, 12, 16; arch of the, 34, 125, 201, 209, 235, 241.
Forum Holitorium, 159, 177.
Forum Julium, 22, 207, 208.
Forum Romanum, 21 fol., 34, 110, 120, 143, 145, 147, 153, 165, 199, 246.
Forum of Trajan, 15, 47, 145, 152, 199.
Forum Transitorium, 157, 212, 255.

S. Francesca Romana, church of, 175.
S. Francesco delle Stimmate, church of, 193.
Frangipani, the, 121, 199, 201.

Gabinius Vettius Probianus, 36.
Gaianum, 87.
S. Galla Patricia, church of, 177.
Gallienus, 32.
Ganymede, statue of, 104.
Gardens, Licinian, 15; of Maecenas, 12; of Sallust, 171.
Gelasius II. See Pope.
Gems and cameos, engraved, usually found near the sites of cemeteries, 94 fol.
Genseric and the Vandals, 74 fol., 119, 455.
Gesù, church of, 263.
S. Giacomo del Colosseo, church of, 89; Scossa-Cavalli, 178.
Gildo, Count, 50.
S. Giorgio in Velabro. See Church.
S. Giovanni, hospital of, 240.
S. Giovanni dei Fiorentini, church of, 264; e Paolo, 254.
S. Giovanni, in Florence, baptistery of, 184.
S. Girolamo degli Schiavoni, church of, 239.
Gladiator, bronze statue of, 66.
Golden House of Nero, 23.
Gordian, the younger, villa of, on the Via Praenestina, 6.
Gothic wars, monument relating to, 50.
Goths, signs of the pillage of Rome by the, 58.
Graecorum Ecclesia et Schola, 176.
Grain Exchange, 34.
Gratianus, 34, 35. See Arch.
Gregorian Chapel, in St. Peter's, 262.
S. Gregorio, church of, 254.
Gregoriopolis, 126 fol.
Gregory the Great, Gregory III., IV., VI., VII., IX., XI., XIII., XVI. See Pope.
Guiscard, Robert, 159 fol.

Hadrian. bust of, 32. See Mausoleum.
St. Hadrian. See Church.

Hadrian I., III. See Pope.
Harpocrates, head of, 196.
Hathor, replica of the sacred cow, 43, 44.
St. Helena, tomb of, 72.
Henry IV., Emperor, 160.
Heracles, torso of, 222.
Heraclius, 118, 119, 122.
Hercules, Farnese, 44; Invictus, statue of, 66; Magnus Custos, bronze statue of, 66; Olivarius, statue of, 39; Victor, 209.
Honorius, 50, 53, 55, 72. See Arch.
Honorius. See Pope.
Horse, bronze, of the Palazzo dei Conservatori, 69.
Horse-tamers, group of, 145, 147, 222, 238.

S. Ignazio, church of, 256.
Innocent II., III., VII., VIII. See Pope.
Inscriptions, of the Einsiedlen Itinerary, 151 fol.; of Benedict, 174 fol.
Isis. See Temple.
Itinerary, Einsiedlen, 142 fol., 174 fol.; of Benedict, 174 fol.

Janus, bronze statue of, 87; temple of, 110.
Janus Quadrifrons, arch of, 125, 201, 211.
Jerusalem, spoils from the temple of, 57.
Johannipolis, 136.
St. John Lateran. See Church, Lateran.
John VII., VIII., IX., X., XI., XII. See Pope.
Julia Domna, 22, 104.
Julian, the Apostate, 48.
Julii Akarii, baths of, 152.
Julius II., III. See Pope.
Juno, temple of, 61, 265.
Jupiter Optimus Maximus, see Temple; Stator, temple of, 18, 121.

Kilns. See Lime-kilns.

Laocoon, replica of, 41; finding of, 211, 222, 223.

INDEX OF SUBJECTS

Lateran, the, 106, 160, 166, 175, 219, 231, 242 fol., 254. See Church, under St. John Lateran.
Lautumiae, 16.
S. Laurentius, in Damaso, church of, 145; in Formoso, 145, 148; of the Ordo, 178; in Pensilis, 147; in Porticu Maiore, 178; in Prasino, 145, 146; on the Via Tiburtina (S. Lorenzo fuori le Mura). See Church.
Leo II., III., IV., V., X., XIII. See Pope.
Leonine wall, 133 fol.
Level of the city, rise in, 53, 54.
Lex Regia, 234.
Liber Politicus of Benedict, 174.
Liber Censuum, 176.
Licinian gardens, 15.
Ligorio, Pirro, 192, 194.
Lime-burners, 180 fol.
Lime-kilns, of Rome, 193 fol.; Palace of Tiberius, 195 fol.; Atrium of Vesta, 196; of Ostia and Porto, 194 fol.
Livia, baths of, on the Palatine, 23; villa of, at Prima Porta, 194; market of, 152.
Loggia of Squarcialupi, 248.
S. Lorenzo fuori le Mura. See Church.
S. Lorenzo, in Panisperna, church of, 246.
Lucca, cathedral of, 184.
S. Lucia de Calcarario (S. Lucia dei Ginnasi), 193; in Selce, 142, 147.
Lucilius Paetus, tomb of, 92.
Lysippus, 8, 87.

Maecenas, gardens of, 12.
Magna Mater, 117.
Maioranus, edict of, 75.
Marble-cutters, 180 fol.; plan of the city, 18.
Marbles, traffic in Roman, 181 fol.; tolerated by public officials, 190 fol.
Marcella, house of, 58; fate of, 59, 60.
Marcelli, church of the, 213.
S. Marcello, church of, 90.
Marcellus. See Theatre.
S. Maria, dell' Anima, church of, 259; Antiqua, 110; in Campitelli, 91; in Cosmedin (see Church); delle Grazie, 91; Liberatrice, 120; Maggiore (see Church); ad Martyres (Pantheon) (see Church); in Monticelli, 165; Nova, 103; Nuova (see Church); della Pace, 204, 260; in Pallara, 256; del Popolo, 204, 259; in Schola Graeca, 122; del Sole, 12; Transpontina, 178; in Trastevere, 152; in Via Lata, 139, 210; in Virgari, 178.
Marinus I., II. See Pope.
Market hall of the Caelian (S. Stefano Rotondo), 34, 37; on the Esquiline, 35.
Marmorarii, 180 fol.
Marmorata, La, 33, 246, 264.
Martin V. See Pope.
S. Martina. See Church.
S. Martino ai Monti, church of, 79.
Mater Matuta, temple of, 12, 39.
Matteo da Castello, architect of Pius IV., 61; of Sixtus V., 85, 240, 252.
S. Mattéo at Salerno, cathedral of, 184.
Mauritius, 106.
Mausoleum, of Augustus, 170, 176, 199; of Constantia, 32; of Hadrian, 8, 87, 151, 186, 189, 208, 210, 256, 262; of the Empress Helena, 246.
Maxentius, 22, 31.
Mediaeval Rome, desolation of, 178 fol.
Mellini, 199.
Meta di Borgo, 178.
Meta Sudans, 30.
S. Michele in Borgo, church of, 117.
Minerva, statue of, 29; temple of, 255.
Minerva Medica (so called), temple of, 95.
Minerva, La. See Church.
Mirabilia Urbis Romae, 175.
Mithras, temple of, 245.
Mole. See Mausoleum.
Moletta, La, 17.
Monte Giordano, 5; de' Cenci, 5.
Moon, temple of the, 17.
Moors of Frassineto, 158.
Moses, fountain of, 239.
Mosileos, the imperial mausoleum of the Decadence, 72.

INDEX OF SUBJECTS

Municipal authorities favor the preservation of monuments, 228 fol.
Museum, Capitoline, 18, 228, 256; al Celio, 13, 90; villa di Giulio III., 13; Torlonia, 105; Vatican, 90, 104, 257; See Palazzo dei Conservatori.
Myron, cow of, 87.

Naevius, Lucius Clemens, house of, 24.
Natural agencies in the demolition of ancient buildings, 7.
Nero, 4; thermae of, 14; set the city on fire, 17 fol.; traces of this fire, 19; Golden House of, 23; Circus of, 32; bust of, 196.
Nerone, Sepoltura di, 158.
Neronis Obeliscus, 177.
St. Nicholas, church of, 169.
Nicolas I., V. See Pope.
S. Nicolaus in Calcaria (S. Nicolo ai Cesarini), church of, 193,
S. Nicolo, in Calcarario, church of, 90; dei Lorenesi, 262.
Nile, figure of, 222.
Normanni, 199.
Norman-Saracenic invasion, 159 fol.; traces of, 162 fol.
Nymphaeum, 151.

Obelisk, of Thothmes III. removed to Rome by Constantine II., 48; of the Vatican, 148, 169, 238; in the Campus Martius, 169, 171 fol.; from the Circus Maximus, 170; from the Mausoleum of Augustus, 170; of the gardens of Sallust, 171; of the temple of Isis, 173; manner of the fall of, 169 fol.; of the Piazza del Popolo, 239.
Obeliscus Neronis, 177.
Octavia. See Porticus.
Odeum, 5, 48.
Oppian, 165.
Oratories of the Lateran destroyed by Sixtus V., 242 fol.
Oratorium Sacrae Crucis, 243 fol.
Ordo Romanus, 174 fol.
Orsini, the, 199.
S. Orso, church of, 151.

Orvieto, cathedral of, 184 fol.
Ostia, 19, 33, 93, 126, 137, 184, 186, 194, 206, 208, 235, 246.

Pactumeii, palace of the, 58.
Pagan edifices converted into Christian churches, 37.
Pagan cults, representation of, in Christian churches, 117 fol.
Palace, of Septimius Severus, 3; of the Caesars in the seventh century, 119, 235; of Augustus on the Palatine, 263 fol.
Palatine, remains of private houses on the, 23; late occupancy of, 119 fol.; desolation of, 199; possessed by the Frangipani, 201.
Palatiolum, 208.
Palazzo, della Cancelleria, 191, 204, 211, 239; dei Conservatori, 13, 222, 231, 232; di Corneto, 191; Farnese, 191, 263; Giraud-Torlonia, 178, 204, 211; del Governo Vecchio, 204; Rospigliosi, 255.
Palilia, 228.
Pallacinae, 147.
Palladium, monastery called, 121.
St. Pancras, church of, 79, 243.
S. Pantaleo ai Monti, church of, 165.
Pantheon, 4, 9, 37, 41, 48, 90, 106, 110 fol., 119, 124, 125, 145, 146, 200, 245, 254, 256, 264.
S. Paolo fuori le Mura. See Church.
Papi, the, 199.
Paschal I., II. See Pope.
Patriarchium, pontifical residence at the Lateran, 242 fol.
St. Paul, tomb of, 129 fol.
St. Paul's without the walls. See Church.
Paul II., III., V. See Pope.
Peace, temple of, 57.
Penates, temple of, 110, 223.
Peregrinorum Castra, 264.
St. Peter, gate of, 145, 177; tomb of, 129 fol., 221, 224; chapel to, 110.
St. Peter's, church of. See Church.
Petrarch, 182.
Petronilla, tomb of, 72.
Phidias, 8, 87.

Philippus, Marcius, 11.
Phocas, 37, 106 fol., 120.
S. Phocas, church of, 122.
Piazza Navona. See Stadium.
Pierleoni, the, 199.
Pietas, shrine of, 10, 159, 177.
S. Pietro, in Montorio; in Vincoli. See Church.
"Pilgrim's Pence," 157.
Pinturicchio, frescoes of, 221, 222.
Pisa, cathedral of, 184.
Pisidius Romulus, 52.
Pius II., IV., V., VI., VII., IX. See Pope.
Poggio Bracciolini, 205 fol.
Pompey. See Theatre.
Pope Alexander VI., 55, 177, 178, 204, 205, 210, 211, 225; Alexander VII., 96, 123, 253, 256; Benedict III., 131, 139; Benedict V., 154; Benedict VI., 155; Benedict VIII., 154; Benedict IX., 155; Benedict XIV., 111, 254; Boniface IV., 37, 110, 112, 115; Boniface VI., 154; Boniface VIII., 98, 234, 243; Boniface IX., 213; Borgia, 133; Caelestinus II., 174, 194; Celestine IV., 213; Christopher I., 155; Clement VII., 133, 222, 225; Clement VIII., 244 fol.; Damasus, 146; Eugenius IV., 112, 203, 204, 207, 213; Formosus, 154, 155; Gelasius II., 184; Gregory the Great, 88, 101; Gregory III., 112; Gregory IV., 126 fol.; Gregory VI., 155; Gregory VII., 154, 160, 162; Gregory IX., 213; Gregory XI., 198; Gregory XIII., 151, 235, 251, 262; Gregory XVI., 155; Hadrian I., 243; Hadrian III., 155; Honorius I., 8, 122, 147; Innocent II., 174; Innocent III., 201; Innocent VII., 213, 219; Innocent VIII., 103, 203, 210, 225; John VII., 120, 219; John VIII., 135 fol., 154; John IX., 155; John X., 154, 155; John XI., 156; John XII., 155; Julius II., 211, 212, 217, 222; Julius III., 36; Leo II., 116; Leo III., 131, 183; Leo IV., 131, 133, 136 fol.; Leo V., 155; Leo X., 211, 213, 217, 222; Leo XIII., 135, 222; Marinus I., 154, 160; Marinus II., 121; Martin V., 204, 206; Nicolas I., 201, 242; Nicolas V., 204, 206, 207, 212, 213; Paschal I., 116; Paschal II., 165; Paul II., 203, 204, 208; Paul III., 33, 96, 191, 225, 228; Paul V., 122, 219, 253, 255; Pius II., 217, 225; Pius IV., 5, 55, 178, 232, 259, 261; Pius V., 227, 239; Pius VI., 104; Pius VII., 189, 194, 218; Pius IX., 55, 189, 219; Romanus, 155; Sergius I., 123; Sergius II., 127, 130; Sergius III., 155; Silverius, 70; Sixtus IV., 55, 203, 204, 209, 217, 222; Sixtus V., 82, 148, 170, 235, 237 fol.; Stephen II., 72, 118; Stephen V., 116; Stephen VI., 155, 159; Sylvester III., 155; Symmachus, 20; Theodore I., 242; Theodore II., 154; Urban VIII., 55, 111, 201, 253, 256; Vigilius, 71; Vitalianus, 112, 124.
Popes destroy ancient monuments to rebuild Christian churches, 206 fol.
Porta Appia, 143; Asinaria, 143, 165; Aurelia, 143, 145; Capena, 31; Collina, 177; Flaminia, 54, 143, 160, 165; Furba, 86; Metroni, 143; Nomentana, 143; Ostiensis, 54; Portuensis, 53, 54; Praenestina, 53, 54, 143; Salaria, 142; Septimiana, 54; Tiburtina, 53, 54, 143, 160, 190; Viminalis, 143.
Porticus, in the Via Bocca della Verità, 176; Crinorum, 177; Eventus Boni, 259; Gallatorum, 176; Maior (Via Sacra), 178; Maximae, of Gratian, 34; Minucia, 177; of Octavia, 28, 176, 186, 187, 208; of Philippus, 176.
Porto. 128, 137, 186, 195, 235, 264.
Postumius, M. Festus, house of, 24.
Praedia Aemiliana, 18.
S. Praesede, church of, 116.
Praetorian camp, 89.
Principia, house of, 58.
S. Prisca, church of, 61.
Prothi Ascesa, 147.
S. Pudens in Vico Patricio, church of, 145, 148.
S. Pudenziana, church of, 246.
SS. Quaranta de Calcarario (S. Francesco delle Stimmate), church of, 193.

SS. Quatro Coronati, church of, 165, 181.
SS. Quirico e Giolitta, church of, 147.
Quirinal, called 'Monte Cavallo,' 147; marble statues on, 166; river gods of, 222.

Ranucci Romano, 180.
Raphael, tapestries of, 217 fol.; frescoes of, 221, 222.
Record office, 37.
Regia, 18, 194.
Regionary Catalogue of the time of Constantine, 48.
Remi Meta, 178.
Rhadagaisus, 50.
Rienzi, Cola di, 234.
S. Rocco, church of, 263.
Roma Vecchia, 104.
Romani, the, 199.
Romanus. See Pope.
Romuli, Sepulcrum, 178, 210.
Romulus, Heroön of, 110, 123, 256.
Rospigliosi gardens, 24.
De Rossi's account, 83, 84.
Rotondo, church of the. See Pantheon.
Ruins of Roman villas, stratification of, 101.

S. Saba, church of, 122.
S. Sabina, church of, 61; garden of, 58.
Sacra Via. See Via.
Sacrae Urbis Templum, 208, 256.
Sallust, gardens of, 58, 89, 261.
S. Salvator de Porticu, church of, 178.
S. Salvatore in Campo, church of, 256.
S. Salvatore in Primicerio, church of, 165.
Sanctus Angelus, 176.
Sanguigni, the, 199.
Saracens, traces of the camp of, 137; in the St. Bernard Pass, 158.
Sarcophagi, used to hold relics of martyrs, 117.
Saturn, temple of, 34, 110.
Savelli, the, 199.
Saviour, church of the, 110.
Schola Graeca, 143.

S. Sebastiano, in Pallara, 91; alla Polveriera, 121.
Secretarium Senatus, 110, 118, 256.
Senate-house, 22, 110, 123, 147, 207, 208.
Sentius Saturninus, G., shrine rebuilt by, 27.
Sepolcro degli Stucchi, 96.
Septa Julia, 208.
Septimius Severus, 18, 28; palace of, 3; restorations of, 22, 28. See Arch.
Septizonium, 121, 152, 201, 235, 239.
Serapeum of Alexandria, 65.
Sergius I., II., III. See Pope.
SS. Sergius and Bacchus. See Church.
Sette Sale, 246.
Severus, architect of Nero, 19.
Severus, Alexander, 28, 191.
Silverius. See Pope.
Silverware, finds of, 63.
S. Silvestro in Capite (St. Sylvester). See Church.
Sinibaldi, the, 199.
Sistine Chapel, 204, 218.
Sixtus IV., V. See Pope.
S. Spirito, hospital of, 204.
Stadium, where now is the Piazza Navona, 5, 48, 146, 199, 246, 262.
Statilian family, Columbaria of, 94.
Statilius Taurus, 11, 199.
Statio Marmorum, 33.
Statuary, removed from pagan places of worship, 36; used as rubble, 41 fol.; condition of, when discovered, 45.
Statues, hiding of bronze, in times of panic, 64 fol.; concealed by magistrates, 65.
Stefaneschi, the 199.
S. Stefano, delle Carozze, 12; Rotondo, 34, 37.
Stephen II., V., VI. See Pope.
Stilicho, 50, 53, 56.
Stratification of ruins, 101.
Streets, condition of, 227.
Studio of Greek sculptors on the Esquiline, 42.
Subura, 143, 145, 147, 201.
Sun, temple of, 199.
S. Susanna, church of, 242.
Sylvester III. See Pope.

INDEX OF SUBJECTS

St. Sylvester. See Church.
Symmachus. See Pope.

Tabernola, 15.
Tapestries of Raphael, 217 fol.
Tarpeian rock, 259.
Temple, of Antoninus and Faustina, 111; Claudius (Caelian), 208, 261; Concord, 110, 206; Craticulae, 177; Dea Dia, 208; Hercules Victor, 209; Hope, 177; Isis, 42, 112, 171, 173, 186, 193, 205, 222, 245; Janus, 110; Juno Regina, 61; Juno (Veii), 265; Jupiter Optimus Maximus, 8, 13, 48, 52, 74, 159, 176, 205, 208, 247, 259 fol.; Jupiter Stator, 18, 121; Mater Matuta, 12, 39; Minerva, 255; Minerva Medica (so called), 95; Mithras, 245; Moon, 17; Peace, 57; Penates, 18; Pietas, 10, 159, 177 ; Romulus, 110, 123, 256; Saturn, 34, 110; Sacrae Urbis, 208, 256; Sun, 199; Venus and Rome, 8, 22, 48, 110, 122, 194, 207, 246; Venus in Calcarario, 245; Venus (gardens of Sallust), 261; Vesta, 18; Vulcan (Ostia), 194.
Temples closed, 35.
S. Teodoro, church of, 264.
Terebinthus, 177.
Theatre, of Balbus, 5; Marcellus, 191, 176, 177, 199; Pompey, 5, 48, 77, 145, 146, 152, 176, 199.
Theoderic, 38, 77 fol., 89, 90, 183.
Theodore I., II. See Pope.
Theodosius, 35, 50. See Arch.
Thermae (see Baths), areas closed for, 14; their building an important factor in the transformation of Rome, 22 fol.; of Agrippa (Commodianae), 145, 146, 193, 245, 259; of Caracalla, 14, 22, 23, 33, 90, 116, 192, 208; of Constantine, 14, 24, 145, 147, 255; of the Decii, 14, 36, 57, 60; of Diocletian, 14, 22, 27, 116, 153, 194, 211, 239, 261; of Nero, 14; of Titus, 14, 23, 32, 36, 262; of Trajan, 14, 23, 32, 36, 145, 148.
Tiber, 33; inundations of, 139 fol.; figure of, 222; treasures thrown into, 225 fol.
Tigellinus, 4, 18.

Titus, 57; house of, 211. See Arch, Thermae.
Tombs, fate of, 91; entrances concealed, 95 fol.; destruction of, 190.
Tombs, of the Apusii, 103; Arruntii, 31; Casal Rotondo, 237; Caecilia Metella, 92, 96, 191, 236 fol.; Gaius Cestius, 96, (Meta Remi), 178; Fabii, 31; on the Via Flaminia, 208; Lucilius Paetus, 92; at the Ponte dell' Arco, 236, 237; Romulus, 178; Alexander Severus, 191; Vergilius Eurysaces, 92; Vibius Marianus, 92. See Sepolcro.
Torre, de' Conti, 201; Fiscale, 82, 162; delle Milizie, 201; di Nona, 41; Pignatarra, 72, 246; dei Schiavi, 7.
Torrecchiano Campo, 199, 202.
Totila, 119, 151.
Trajan, arch of, 31; channel of, 33; house of, 57; column of, 109, 125, 145, 146, 148, 166, 238. See Forum, Thermae.
Treasures, concealed at the sack of 1527, 224 fol.
Tribunus Voluptatum, 78.
Triumph of Diocletian, 49 fol.
Tulliola, 103.
Turcius Asterius Secundus, 63.
Turris Chartularia, 121, 201.

Ugolini house, 5.
Umbilicus Romae, 145.
Urban VIII. See Pope.

Vacca, Flaminio, extracts from memoirs of, 5, 39, 90, 192, 194, 259.
Valens. See Arch.
Valentinian I., 33; bridge of (Ponte Sisto), 34, 246; prohibited sacrifices, 35. See Arch.
Valentinian III., 74 fol.
Valerius Severus, 59.
Vassalecti, 180.
Vatican, the, 128, 133, 175. See Museum, St Peter's.
Vatican district included in the city proper, 132.
Veii, 186.
Venantius Fortunatus, 109.

Venus, Venus and Rome. See Temple.
Vergilius Eurysaces, tomb of, 92.
Verus, Lucius, statue of, 104.
Vespasian, Lex Regia of, 234.
Vesta, temple of, 18; statue of, 196.
Vestals, house of, 121, 122, 196, 264.
Via Appia, 31, 103, 105, 137, 194; Aurelia, 16; Clodia, 158; Collatina, 16; Cornelia, 32; Labicana, 16, 72; Latina, 96, 160, 194; Nomentana, 20, 32; Nova, 31; Praenestina, 6; Sacra, 34, 36, 52, 110, 120, 153, 178, 191, 211; Salaria Vetus, 15, 65, 151; Salaria Nova, 15; Tiburtina, 33; Triumphalis, 177, 178. See Clivus, Vicus.
S. Vibiana, church of, 116, 256.
Vibius Marianus, tomb of, 92.
Victory, statue of, 48.
Vicus Capitis Africae, 151; Patricius, 240; Portae Viminalis, 240; Tuscus, 153.

Vigilius. See Pope.
Vigna Barberini, 19, 121; Barberini-Spithoever, 89; Ceccarelli, 116; Grimani (Barberini), 90; Maciocchi, 57; Moroni, 95; Torlonia, 57.
Villa Corsini-Pamfili, 16; Giulia, 191, 263; di Giulio III. (museo), 13; Gordianorum (Via Praenestina), 6, 7; Livia, 194; Quintiliorum, 103 fol.; Voconiorum, 105.
Vitalianus. See Pope.
S. Vitalis in Vico Longo, church of, 145, 148, 192.
Vitiges, siege of, 79, 89, 115.
Volusianus, Rufus, 33.
Vulcan, temple of (at Ostia), 194.

Wall, Leonine, 133 fol.; of Aurelian, 15.

Zmaragdus, 109.

II. INDEX OF PASSAGES AND INSCRIPTIONS CITED

A. AUTHORS

AMMIANUS MARCELLINUS

	PAGE
XVI. 10,	47

ST. AUGUSTINE
Sermo cv de verbis Evang. Luc.

X. 13,	65

CASSIODORIUS
Variae

vii. 13,	38
iii. 10,	38

CLAUDIANUS
De VI. Consulatu Honorii

42,	65

CODEX BARBERINIANUS

xxx. 25,	152

CODEX THEODOSIANUS

x. Tit. 17,	92

DION CASSIUS

xliii. 49,	11

FRONTINUS

i. 13,	80

HORACE
Satires

	PAGE
I. viii. 8 fol.,	15

ST. JEROME
Letters

xlviii.,	59
xcvi.,	59

LIBER PONTIFICALIS

Gregorius, iv. 38,	126
Vol. II., 145, xxii.,	131
Vol. II., 145, xxiii.,	139
Vol. II., 225, 235, 240, 248, 270, 275,	155
Vol. II., 258,	156

LIVY

xxiv. 46,	16
xxvi. 27,	16

MON. GERM. SCR. LANG.

Vol. I., p. 53,	155
Vol. I., p. 483,	156
Vol. VI., p. 358,	157

INDEX OF INSCRIPTIONS

PRUDENTIUS
Contra Sym.

	PAGE
i. 501-505,	35

PLINY THE ELDER
Historia Naturalis

	PAGE
vii. 36, 121,	10

PROCOPIUS
de Bello Gothico

	PAGE
i. 19,	79, 145
ii. 3,	83
iv. 22,	87

SUETONIUS

	PAGE
Octav. 29,	11

TACITUS
Annales

	PAGE
xv. 43,	19

VENANTIUS FORTUNATUS
Carmina

	PAGE
iii. 23,	109

ZOSIMUS

	PAGE
v. 45,	57

B. INSCRIPTIONS

	PAGE
Benevento, inscription found at,	65
Brick stamp of Theoderic,	78
Capua, inscription found at,	65

Corpus Inscriptionum Latinarum

	PAGE
i. 285,	112
p. 415,	194
vi. 472,	153
562,	153
773,	153
vi. 916,	153
1014,	153, 231
1016,	153
1173,	33
1178,	1 2
1187,	50
1188-90,	53
1191,	152
1472,	153
1651,	36
1658,	36
1663,	36
1664,	37
1703,	61
1708,	153
1711,	153
1728 a,	151
1730,	50
14, 647,	20

Ephemeris Epigraphica

	PAGE
iii. p. 287,	21

DE ROSSI: *Inscr. Chr. Urbis Romae*

	PAGE
Vol. II., p. 212,	156
p. 215,	155, 156
p. 347,	136

FABRETTI: *Inscriptiones Domesticae*

	PAGE
p. 721, no. 431,	20

MARINI: *Inscriptiones alb.*

	PAGE
x.,	194
Notizie degli Scavi: 1880, p. 53,	51